Classic CAJUN
Culture & Cooking

Revised Edition

Lucy Henry Zaunbrecher

PHOTOGRAPHERS

Cover Photographer:

Tom Gibbs was educated at NLU, majoring in journalism. He also attended the Brooks Institute of Photography in Santa Barbara, California, where he majored in commercial photography. During the Vietnam conflict, he served in the United States Navy as a photographer's assistant. He now does commercial work for local, out-of-town and out-of-state firms and individuals. He specializes in both location and studio photography, tailoring to each client. He lives in Monroe, Louisiana.

Cajun Culture Photographer and short cultural stories by Philip Gould.

Philip Gould is a cultural documentary photographer living near Lafayette. His books include *Cajun Music and Zydeco, Louisiana—A Land Apart*, and *Les Cadiens d'asteur (Today's Cajuns)*. His work has also appeared in numerous national magazines.

Cover picture is of Mrs. Lucy in the kitchen with her granddaughter, Lucy Suzanne McKenzie.

ISBN: 0-9640748-0-X

1st Printing	July, 1994
2nd Printing	January, 1995
3rd Printing	July, 1996
4th Printing	June, 1997
5th Printing	May, 1999
6th Printing	October, 1999

Printed in the USA by

WIMMER
The Wimmer Companies
Memphis
1-800-548-2537

Merci Beaucoup

Chef Hans and Joe Travis, my friends who got me away from cooking to inspire the writing of all my favorite recipes for you to enjoy.

Merci bien to the work of my sisters-in-law who were generous with their recipes.

Bien merci, Msgr. Jules O. Daigle, for helping inform me about the history of the Cajun people.

Merci to Freddie Strange, who bore with me through the tears of this experience.

For everything else, mille merci to Lonnie Walters, Jennifer Morgan, Lisa Holdiness for knowing how to keep me on track to get to print even if they can't do any cooking.

Merci, merci, merci Daryl and Lee Ann Riser for allowing me to be your ''slave driver.''

Merci, Maw Maw Sue, for the beautiful setting. (You, too, Poppie.)

Thank you, Harry Zaunbrecher (Le General).

INTRODUCING CLASSIC CAJUNS

Grand mere

Frozine Foreman Richard
1880-1950

Mama

Eloise R. Henry
Eloise Richard Henry
1910-1991

Lucy Henry Zaunbrecher
Lucy Henry Zaunbrecher
1938-

Lucy Suzanne McKenzie
1991-

This cookbook is for my granddaughter, Lucy Suzanne McKenzie.
Grandmere handed down her cooking to my Mama and she handed
down her cooking to me. With this cookbook, Lucy, preserve our
beautiful Gueydan culture and cooking.

Mon Cherie, let your kitchen hand our cooking on down to your
petits enfants.

Je t'aime,
Maw Maw Lucy

GETTING TO KNOW MRS. LUCY

Most of my childhood in Gueydan was spent in the kitchen watching my mother cook three meals a day. Through watching my mother cook and helping her prepare the ingredients, I learned the French Acadien (Cajun) style of cooking. This good Cajun food has always been and always will be a part of me.

Every Cajun has the love of cooking.

As a child, I discovered that in South Louisiana, we had access to the wildlife of the area and the seafood of the Gulf. We raised our own chickens and grew our own vegetables. We had basic down to earth living.

To this day, I always use Watkins flavorings and black pepper because that is what my mother always used. Her first cousin, Mr. Foreman, was a traveling salesman. In those days, we did not go to town often, nor did we have many visitors, so we welcomed his monthly visits. My mother purchased her spices, mixes and seasonings from him and he also enjoyed a good meal with us. Today, I order my Watkins products from a small catalog.

Fais do does were always memorable. My parents and their friends would dance while I layed on top of a table nearby or sat next to them. As I got older, I joined the dancers on the dance floor. Because I was too young then for boyfriends, I would dance with girlfriends. It is still very common in South Louisiana for women to dance together.

My parents, Elbey Henry and Eloise Richard Henry, were of true Cajun heritage and only spoke French to each other and to me. (When my brother and sister came along, they spoke English to them.) When I started school, I could not speak any English. By the end of the year, Madeline Broussard, who taught the French-speaking children, had taught me English.

French was not allowed to be spoken on the school grounds for many years. I believe this helped lead to the diminishment of the Cajun heritage as I knew it as a child. Now, Cajun French is being taught to students in some schools.

When I was 20, I married my childhood sweetheart, Harry Zaunbrecher, who was one of 12 children. Harry's grandparents came over from Germany and settled in Robert's Cove. When Harry and I returned from our honeymoon, Harry's mother gave me her kitchen as a welcoming present.

From that day until I moved into my own home, I began preparing three meals a day for four adults and five children. I did all of the grocery shopping, budgeting and planning for the meals. This started my career as a Cajun cook.

I always use my Magnalite set of pots to cook in. I got a full set from my Uncle Bill as a graduation present. He is also a good cook and definitely knew a good set of pots. Little did he know at that time that I would still be using the same pots 35 years later!!

When I say salt and pepper to taste, I mean: use one teaspoonful of salt and one teaspoonful of pepper. Then taste. If the seasoning is okay for you, then do not add more. If not, add according to your taste.

I have washed a lot of dishes in my life and that is why I now use a lot of Pam spray. It makes the dishwashing much easier.

Harry and I moved to Jones in northeast Louisiana when I was 24. After we moved, I discovered how priceless an inheritance my parents had left me. To my amazement, I found out that the Mason-Dixon line was actually in Alexandria. I had grown up believing that everyone, especially in Louisiana, was Cajun.

Wrong!!

Jones is a whole new world from Gueydan. The people were different, the cultures were different and the language was different. During my life, I have experienced the best of two worlds without leaving the state.

Over the years, I have watched the Cajun heritage slowly diminish. Through this cookbook, I hope to share part of my wonderful heritage. I hope this will help contribute to the survival of our most honorable Cajun culture through its heart and soul — our cooking.

COOKING THE CAJUN WAY

Cajuns specialize in plain, simple meals which are filling and tasty for country folk. They take cooking and foods seriously and take great pride in them.

Cajuns don't make a lot of different salads because they seldom eat them. In the few salads they do make, they never peel the tomatoes or remove their seeds. Also, they always season their meats before putting them in the pot to cook.

Appetizers are also rare in Cajun kitchens. Very seldom, if ever, is an appetizer served since the Cajuns fear it would only ruin their appetite before a good meal.

Cajuns love sweets but rarely eat dessert after a hearty meal.

Cajun cooking may be time consuming, but it is well worth what you put into it. It has to be. Cajuns love eating their foods as much as they love preparing them.

To truly understand Cajun food, you have to understand the Cajun people. That's why I've incorporated photos and stories of the people throughout this book.

I've also provided the following essay on the Cajun people in an effort to further understanding of their unique culture.

CAJUNS — WHO THEY ARE

To the uninitiated, a Cajun is a crude ignorant backwoodsman who speaks little or no English. He makes his living fishing, trapping or farming a few acres of land and his principal interests are boozing, eating and having a good time.

Perhaps there are such people in Acadiana, but they are an infinitesimal minority and are in no way characteristic of the Cajun people.

Instead, Cajuns have a long and proud heritage on this continent. This heritage began in 1604 when the first French settler colonized Nova Scotia. Much like America's first colonists, they fought to civilize a new world, bringing the culture and language of France to their adopted land.

England gained control of Nova Scotia with the Treaty of Utrech in 1713 and life became unbearable for the Cajuns. As French Catholics living under the rule of English Protestants, the Cajuns found themselves despised and persecuted. Between 6,000 and 7,000 were deported to the American colonies. However, most of these colonies also had laws prohibiting Catholics to live within their borders, so life didn't get much better.

Others sought refuge in the Caribbean or among the Indians of the American wilderness. Others, deported to England, eventually found their way to France.

Refugees from all these groups eventually found their way to Louisiana. There, they founded their own communities. In a climate unlike any they'd known before, surrounded by plants and animals for which they had no names in their language, the Cajuns created a new language and a new culture. It even became necessary to create a new way of cooking since many of the ingredients they'd known were unavailable — replaced by the abundant seafood and game of south Louisiana. Small, family-owned stores and meat markets still exist in southwest Louisiana in testimony to the impact this had on the lives of the Cajuns.

When the Acadiens came into the bayou country from New Orleans, the Indians here could not pronounce "Acadien." Therefore, the name "Cajun" was adopted because it was easier to pronounce.

However, the words Cajun and Acadien do not have the same meaning. The word Cajun applies only to those whose Acadien ancestors came to Louisiana after the eviction of 1755. The broader term, Acadien, applies to all the descendants of the original Acadiens, regardless of where they live. Thus, all Cajuns are Acadiens, but not all Acadiens are Cajuns.

Many thousands of Acadiens live in different parts of the United States and Canada. These are not Cajuns. By extension, the title of Cajun is properly applied to those people (regardless of national origin) who have intermarried with Cajuns and have been absorbed into the Cajun culture and speak the Cajun langauge. This is why my husband is classified as a Cajun even though his name is Zaunbrecher and he is of German descent.

Today, historians agree that the culture the Cajuns developed is one of the most unique and impressive in the world. They also agree that the Cajuns have played a significant role in American history as they struggled to survive.

Throughout this rebirth of Acadiana, the Cajuns stuck together. They minded their own business, kept apart from the rest of the world and supported each other.

In the 20th century, oil brought riches to the Cajuns. Yet even this couldn't change them much.

Today, they are as they always were: fun-loving, God-fearing, hard-working. Over a million of these French-speaking people exist in our country today, a tribute to their determination and the power of the human will.

In spite of the tribulations they've endured, today's Cajuns still maintain a joie-de-vivre and a live-and-let-live attitude which is admired by all who know them. They are ready with a smile, a joke and a handshake for anyone willing to accept it. They'll give you the shirt off their back or the beer out of their glass.

That is who a Cajun is.

CAJUNS AND NOT CREOLES

I've often been asked to explain the difference between Cajuns and Creoles.

This basically comes down to a question of style. Creole cooking is a more sophisticated, city cousin of Cajun cooking. Both come from the same roots.

Both Cajun and Creole cuisines were found and brought together by their French roots, livened with spices from Spain, inspired by African vegetables, Caribbeanized by West Indian hands, laced with black pepper and pork by the Germans, infiltrated with potatoes by the Irish, blasted with tomatoes and garlic by the Italians and also touched in a small way by the Swiss, Dutch, Malayans and Malaysians.

What a complex taste!

The Creoles have sauces and delicious soups beyond describing. Their brunches are luscious. The "Haute" (up town) manner of wining and dining reflects the dignified French social groups of Creoles.

Many different courses are also served.

The French from France married with the Spanish and their direct descendants were Creoles. However, many ethnic groups were brought in, diluting the Creole race. New Orleans is the "Heart" of Creole country, the same as Breaux Bridge and Lafayette are the "Heart" of Cajun Country.

Classic
CAJUN

Table of Contents

First You Make A Roux

First you make a roux! Sound familiar?

What is a roux? Well, to me, it is the foundation of many Cajun dishes.

A roux is a mixture of flour and oil slowly cooked to a perfect uniform brown color. Most of the rouxs consist of equal parts of flour and oil (one cup oil plus one cup flour).

I always allow the oil to get hot before adding the flour — this speeds up the cooking time of the roux. A medium high heat is recommended. The slower the roux is cooked, the better the flavor. Beginners should use a medium heat and only experts should cook a roux on high heat.

As soon as the required color is formed, turn off the heat and add the sliced or chopped onions to the roux. Since the onions cannot burn, it will cool off the roux so that the desired color is retained and the roux will not burn nor get darker. However, you must continue to stir the roux even though the heat is off.

Some dishes do not require onions. In that case, remove the roux from the heat and continue to stir until it has cooled. You may also place the pot in cold water to help cool it down.

Learning the process of making a roux is half the challenge of becoming a good Cajun cook.

Basic Roux

1 cup oil
1 cup flour
Water for gumbo or gravy (2-3 quarts for
gumbo; 1 quart for gravy)

Pour oil into a thick, heavy pot, stirring constantly; add flour, being careful not to burn. If you notice some black specks in your roux, just throw it away and start anew. The specks give it a bitter taste which, as far as I know, cannot be remedied.

A whisk is a wonderful tool to use in preparing a roux but be careful of the edges around the pot — use a spoon to stir on the sides occasionally to scrape loose the flour.

Cook on medium high heat until the desired color has been obtained. A dark roux of dark chocolate color is required to use for gumbos, stews and sauce piquantes. A lighter roux which resembles the color of peanut butter is required for ettoufees or light gravies.

Once the right color is obtained, add the required amount of water, stirring constantly. Bring to a fast boil, then lower the heat to a slow boil until the right thickness is obtained.

A roux can be made and stored in a refrigerator for months. If you keep it to be used later, do not add any water but continue to stir after the heat has been turned off until it cools down.

It will be very thick and pasty. Store in a covered container. When needed, remove the amount you need and stir into a quart of boiling water until it is all dissolved.

Roux is definitely not to be eaten alone, but is absolutely necessary for most Cajun specialties. Roux is a big asset to a dish as it is used as a thickener and a flavoring agent.

In a Cajun kitchen, herbs, seasonings and spices are used to enhance the taste of the main ingredient (fish, pork, beef, poultry, etc.) A Cajun always pours off excess fat in a dish to "de-glace" the pan. (Pour in a little water and scrape loose the browned part to add flavor and make a gravy.)

GUMBO

Gumbo is the Cajun's favorite dish for family and friends. It is very typical of a Cajun to say, "Ya'll come over and we'll make a big pot of gumbo." Gumbo is a one-dish, main course meal.

Every year, we attended Christmas midnight mass. Then, after the services, we always went home to a pot of chicken gumbo which my mother had prepared before we went to church.

So, as the song says, "Jambalaya, crawfish pie, file' gumbo!" Gumbo always reflects a celebration or a good time with friends or relatives or both. That is why the gumbo pot is a big one and every kitchen is equipped with one of those.

The following recipe comes from an interview in "Les Acadien D'Asteur" by Philip Gould.

You start with some oil in your pot. And then you make your roux with some flour, white flour, you know. Then, you peel your onion. You cut it fine, fine. Then when your roux is browned, then you take your onion and you brown it with your roux. Then, if you want to make a gallon of gumbo, you put about a gallon water in it to boil.

Then, you brown your chicken on the side. And then you put your chicken in it, into your gumbo. And you let it simmer for about an hour and a half, or an hour. On a low fire, you want to put it. If it's an old hen, it takes maybe like two hours to make your gumbo. And if it's a young chicken, it doesn't take as long. And then, instead of putting in chicken, you can just put seafood if you want. It's just as good and maybe better. But that, you have to put in at the very end, just before it's finished.

Then you put in your salt, your black pepper and your cayenne. You season it like you like it. You can put red peppers or green peppers, or both. Like you want. That's up to you. Then, you taste it to see if it's seasoned enough. That's when you're ready, about 15, 20 minutes before putting out your fire, you chop your parsley and your onion tops. And you put them in there, in your gumbo, just about 15 minutes before your gumbo is cooked. And then, that's all. Your gumbo is ready! Then it's all right. When you're ready to serve it in your bowls, you put your file'. Then you eat it with rice in your bowls.

GUMBO

BEEF CATTLE DRIVE

In the little town of Scott, there is a sign which reads "Here the West begins." That sign is a proud reminder of the days when from Scott to the Sabine River there were numerous "Vacheries" (cattle drives) where Acadiens and other pioneers grazed their herds of long-horned Spanish cattle in a vast, sparsely settled prairie region which was really the "Wild West" long before the trail drivers of the Lone Star State of Texas gained fame as heroes of the uncharted plains.

This scene is reproduced each year as men along with friends and family drive their cattle across the Intracoastal Canal at Forked Island or out of the marshlands near Gueydan. The cattle are driven south to graze during the warm months and brought back inland for the winter where they will be fed and kept out of the cold till the next spring.

After a long hard drive, everyone gathers around to have a few "cool ones" and relive the experiences of the day.

BEEF

Smothered Steak

½ cup oil
4 pounds chuck steak or round steak
  salt & pepper to taste
1 large onion, sliced thinly
1 pint water

Beef was always part of our diet. We ate it practically every day at one of our meals. Of course, on Friday, Catholics were not allowed to eat meat. However, after Vatican II, we were allowed to do so. I was pleased about this mainly because good seafood was not available in North Louisiana. (New freezing methods now make good seafood available anywhere.) This is a good dish to prepare for a simple meal when a lot of hungry men are to be served.

Line bottom of heavy Dutch oven or deep skillet with oil. Heat until hot and add seasoned meat. Brown on one side then turn on other side and brown well. The meat may stick on the bottom of the pot, but that is okay because it makes for a better gravy. Cook on medium high heat, turning over occasionally, adding dabs of water as you turn. Just before meat is cooked, add sliced onions and cook until they are done, approximately 20 minutes. The meat and onions will be done at the same time. Add a small amount of water to form gravy. Serve over rice. Serves 6.

NOTES

_____

_____

_____

_____

_____

_____

Hannah Jane's Spaghetti

1 pound ground beef
1 pound ground pork
1 medium chopped bell pepper
1 medium onion, chopped
2 stalks chopped celery
1 cup soft bread crumbs
1 beaten egg
1 teaspoon basil leaves
1 tablespoon salt
1 tablespoon pepper
2 minced garlic cloves
2 cups flour
1 cup oil

Spaghetti was seldom served at our home when I was growing up. I guess my parents never cultivated a taste for anything unless it was served with rice. However, a very dear friend of mine, Hannah Jane Hardee, tops all the spaghetti cookers. She was generous enough to relinquish her recipe to me.

Mix first 11 ingredients in a large bowl. Shape into balls at least 2 inches in diameter. Roll meatballs in flour and brown in hot oil until done Set aside.

Sauce
2 6 ounce cans tomato paste
½ cup oil
¼ cup sugar
2 quarts water

Brown tomato paste and oil over low heat for 2 hours. Stir occasionally to prevent sticking. After it is browned to the color of a roux (deep golden brown), add water and sugar and simmer. Add meatballs, cover and simmer for about 3 hours. Remove cover for the last hour so as to thicken the gravy. Serve over spaghetti which has been prepared according to package. Serves 4-6.

The "B" Roast

My older daughter, Barbara, claims that she cannot cook. That is only because she had never done much more than microwave a baked potato. Since she married, she has had to prepare several meals, but that is only because her husband, Bernard, has taught her some of his favorite dishes, which she prepares very well. This is one of my favorites, which I have enjoyed eating with them.

1   3-4 pounds boneless rump roast
1   lemon, juice and slices
½   cup white wine
¼   cup Worchestershire sauce
1   tablespoon minced garlic
1   tablespoon Greek seasoning
    salt and pepper to taste
4-5 slices of bacon
1   10¾ ounce can Cream of Mushroom Soup
1   cup mushroom stems & pieces
½   cup water

Place roast in a shallow pan. Season roast with salt and pepper. Sprinkle juice of lemon on top and also drop slices on top of roast. Add wine, Worchestershire sauce, garlic and Greek seasoning. Marinate overnight in refrigerator. The following morning, in a cast-iron dutch oven cook 4-5 slices of bacon until done and remove from pot. Take roast out of pan. Set marinade aside. Brown roast well on both sides in hot bacon grease. Add the marinade, mushrooms, mushroom soup, bacon slices and water. Cover and cook at 375 degrees in oven for 2 hours. Remove and carve. Serve the gravy over rice. Serves 6.

Kirk's Brisket

5-7 **pounds beef brisket, trimmed well of fat**
salt and pepper to taste
Louisiana red hot sauce to taste
¼ **cup wine vinegar (approximately)**
1 **small bag charcoal**
2 **cans Dawn's Mushroom Steak Sauce**
½ **pound fresh mushrooms, sliced**
1 **large sliced onion**
1 **large cut-up bell pepper**
1 **head of garlic, chopped**

Season the brisket well with salt, pepper and wine vinegar. Slit to make a pocket on one side. Stuff onions, bell pepper and garlic inside the pocket. Secure with toothpicks. Set aside and allow to remain in refrigerator overnight. Heat the charcoals in bar-b-que pit until they are real hot. Set brisket on rack and brown real well on both sides, 10 minutes per side. Put in pan sprayed with PAM. Pour steak sauce over brisket and sprinkle sliced mushrooms over sauce. Cover with foil. Bake at 200 degrees for 4-5 hours. Slice and pour gravy over meat before serving. Serves 6-8.

Who says you can't learn from the younger generation. I have recently learned how to prepare this wonderful meat from my nephew, Kirk. We were entertaining some friends from Belgium and some family members from North Louisiana so I picked this as the entree. It is very economical when feeding a multitude of people and can't be any tastier.

Cabbage Rolls

I wish I had a dollar for the many times I have prepared these. My husband really thinks these are great. And they are! I usually prepare them one day and bake them the next day for a meal of leisure. Seems like they taste better that way.

1   large head of cabbage
2   quarts of water
1   small fryer, cut into pieces
1   pound ground beef
1   cup oil
¾   cup chopped onion
½   cup chopped bell pepper
½   cup chopped celery
¼   cup chopped green onion tops
3   cups cooked rice
    salt and pepper to taste
    Louisiana Red Hot Sauce

Core cabbage and pull leaves apart to have as many whole ones as possible. Blanch cabbage leaves in boiling water for 2-3 minutes. Remove from water and allow to cool. Be careful not to tear leaves. Boil cut up fryer pieces in water until meat is cooked. Remove from water and allow to cool. Tear meat apart from bones, set aside. Brown ground beef, onions, bell pepper and celery in oil. Add the chicken meat, green onion tops and cooked rice. Mix thoroughly. Salt and pepper to taste. Take a cabbage leaf and put the meat mixture by tablespoon to fill the leaf partially. Roll the leaf with the mixture inside to resemble a big cigar. Lay in a baking pan that has been sprayed with PAM. Stuff all the cabbage leaves. Lay in the pan, cover with foil and bake at 350 degrees for 30 minutes. When serving rolls, sprinkle dabs of red hot sauce on top of each roll. If any of the stuffing is left unrolled, it can be used as a dressing or a stuffing for another dish. Serves 4.

If I am in a hurry and do not have time to roll leaves, I layer the cabbage leaves and the meat mixture, alternating one after the other until all are used. Then I cover the baking dish and bake as a casserole at 350 degrees for 20 minutes.

NOTES

BOUCHERIE

Boucheries are still popular in south Louisiana as a social activity as well as a means of avoiding high meat prices. Many families and friends gather to do this.

The actual activities of the day go as follows:

After they kill and clean the pig, the head is removed and used to make hog's head cheese. Naturally, they eat the cheese a little as they go. The pig's feet are boiled and pickled. The blood is caught in a pan with salt. They mix that with some meat and green onions to make red boudin. The pig's liver and trimmings make the white boudin. The intestines are cleaned to make the boudin and sausage casings.

Now, your hams and other lean parts are used to make salt meat and fresh sausage. They put that in jars and save it for the long months. It's got to be used over the long run.

They cut up the skin and outer layer of fat and cook it in a big pot to make cracklins and hog lard.

Ribs are used to make fricassee'. The meat from the ribs is removed in the slab and made into bacon.

The backbone and kidneys are used to make a fricassee' de rentier. They feed that to all the people who help with the boucherie that day.

The tongue is cleaned, stuffed with garlic and onions and cooked as a roast. The stomach, or chaudin, is stuffed with rice dressing and baked.

Now, there are some people who will fry the brain and lungs in corn meal.

All this is done that day.

Boucherie Menu
Hog's Head Cheese
Boudin
Gumbo
Country Ribs
Cole Slaw
Sweet Potato Balls
Cracklin' Corn Bread
Bread Pudding with Whiskey Sauce
Les Oreilles de Cochon
Beverages: Beer

PORK

Smothered Pork Chops

6 pork chops, at least ½ inch thick
¼ inch oil in bottom of pot
salt and pepper to taste
1 pint of water
1 cup finely chopped onion

Pork was my favorite meat; therefore, I learned many ways to cook it. This was the quickest way to cook pork and it is very tasty. Pork was served often at my house, mainly because we had easy access to buy hogs and butcher our own pork. Thank God we did not raise them because if we did, I do not believe I would have enjoyed it as much.

Brown seasoned pork chops in heavy pot, turning over several times, allowing them to stick to the bottom of the pot. Add small amounts of water every time the bottom sticks. Once they are browned, add chopped onions and cook until onions wilt. Add about one-forth cup of water and simmer until done, approximately 15-20 minutes. This will make a pretty gravy. Serve over rice. Serves six.

Fried Pork Chops

Another of my favorites. Do not use chops that are thick as it will require more time to cook them.

4 pork chops, ¼ inch thick
2 eggs, beaten
½ cup flour
1½ cups oil
salt and pepper to taste

Season chops with salt and pepper. Dip into beaten eggs. Dredge, coating both sides well. Run through flour and coat both sides. Drop in hot oil 400 degrees and fry until golden brown on both sides (about 10 minutes for each side). Serves four.

I serve this with creamed potatoes or rice dressing.

Pork Roast

1	pork roast (4 pounds)
¼	cup finely chopped onion
4	cloves of garlic, finely chopped
1	teaspoon of salt
½	teaspoon of pepper
¼	cup of oil
2	cups of water
	salt and pepper to taste

This was the ultimate! Even though my mother cooked beef roast, we also had a small pork roast on the side. Of course, you know what was eaten first. This and baked sweet potatoes never failed to impress anyone, especially me.

Combine chopped onion and garlic in a small dish. Season with salt and pepper. Cut slit in the middle of roast and stuff all the onion mixture inside. Season outside of roast with salt and pepper. Heat the oil in a heavy roasting pot. Place the roast in the pot. Brown all sides, adding small amounts of water occasionally. After roast is browned on all sides, add the rest of the water and cover. Cook on low heat about three hours. This also makes a wonderful gravy. Serve over rice. Serves six to eight.

I also cook my beef roasts in this same manner. Just follow the above directions, using beef instead of pork.

NOTES

Boudin

I first remember making boudin when I was about five years old. My parents used cut cow horns to stuff the casing with because there were no sausage stuffers in those days. I bothered my parents to help make boudin so badly that my father made a special little horn for me to use. (I still have it in my possession.) But then I grew older and the boudin making days became more like work than play. I knew that my parents made the best boudin in the world.

1 pig's head, split in half, discard the eyes, nose and ears
1 pork roast, about six pounds
1 gallon of water in a large pot
2 cups chopped onions
2 large bunches of green onions, chopped
1 bunch parsley, chopped
10 cups cooked rice
 salt and pepper to taste
 sausage casing, washed well

Boil meat until it is tender and well cooked, about 1½ hours. Save broth. Discard skin from head. Take meat off of the bone. Grind all meat. Put in a very large container. Add onions, green onions, parsley and salt and pepper. Add enough broth to make real moist (about 1½ cup). If it is too dry, you can add more broth at any time. Add cooked rice (cold rice does better). Mix meat mixture with rice very well. Stuff dressing into casings using a sausage maker. Tie ends of the casings. When ready to eat, bring pot of water to a full boil. Turn heat completely off. Add boudin and cover. The boudin should be submerged in the water. Allow to steam for 10 minutes. Serve hot or cold.

To freeze boudin, put in water and allow to freeze that way as it will retain its taste better. Completely thaw to cook. This recipe makes a lot of boudin because it is not a dish that you would prepare only small portions of.

When I have any left-over boudin from a meal, I fry it in a covered skillet with some hot oil in it—enough to cover the bottom of the pot. This is also very good.

Andouille

5 **pounds of pork stomach**
10 **pounds of pork butt, cut into ½ inch cubes**
½ **pound of fresh garlic, minced**
1 **ounce of cayenne pepper**
½ **ounce of black pepper**
½ **cup of curing salt**
¼ **cup monosodium glutamate sausage casing**

This is more or less a New Orleans used product. But since I have learned to use it, my freezer is never without it. It definitely adds flavor and zest to a dish.

Rinse pork stomach in salty water, cut open and remove all fat. Grind coarsely in food processor or food grinder. Mix all ingredients together and stuff into casing using a sausage stuffer. Yields 15 pounds of fresh Andouille. Use in gumbos or jambalayas.

If a smoker is available, smoke at 120 degrees to 150 degrees for approximately 4-6 hours.

NOTES

Pork Chop Jambalaya

This is a very simple way to fix jambalaya. It is a delicious dish that any vegetable can accompany.

2 pounds pork chops
  salt and pepper
¼ inch oil in bottom of pot
1 cup chopped onions
¾ cup chopped bell pepper
¼ cup chopped celery
1 cup water
4 cups cooked rice
1½ cup chopped green onion tops

Brown pork chops that have been seasoned to taste. Remove chops from pot. Sauté onions, bell pepper, and celery in oil that chops were browned in. Remove all oil from the pot that you can and add a small amount of water to form a gravy. Put chops back into the pot. Cook on medium heat for about 20 minutes. Add cooked rice and onion tops and stir well. Cover and simmer for 10 minutes. Serves 4.

NOTES

Old Style Pork Jambalaya

3 **pounds pork ribs**
or
2 **pounds pork chops**
Salt and pepper to taste
¼ **inch oil in bottom of pot**
1 **cup chopped onions**
¾ **cup chopped bell pepper**
¼ **cup chopped celery**
3 **cups raw rice**
4 **cups water**
½ **cup chopped green onions**
2 **heaping tablespoons sugar**
2 **cups water**

This is the way my mother always cooked her pork jambalaya. The caramelized sugar gave it a beautiful color and wonderful flavor. This is my favorite jambalaya.

Brown seasoned chops in oil, remove from pot and set aside. Sauté onions, bell pepper and celery in oil that chops or ribs have been browned in. Remove as much oil as possible. Return chops to pot and remove from heat. In another pot, caramelize sugar, stirring constantly, until sugar reaches a dark brown color, do this on a low flame. Be patient, it takes a while. Remove from heat and add 2 cups water slowly. Bring back to a boil until all caramelized sugar is dissolved with water. Pour the mixture into the pot with pork and sautéed vegetables. Bring to a boil. Add onion tops, raw rice and 4 cups water. Stir well, making sure rice has enough water in it to cook thoroughly. Cook on medium heat until all water boils out of it. Cover and simmer for 15 minutes. Serve hot. Serves 4-6.

Stuffed Chaudin à Vermilion

This is one of the specialty dishes of Cajuns. Nothing was discarded when a boucherie was made. The stomach of a hog was highly valued and enjoyed by everyone. I never did cultivate a taste for it but the stuffing is a favorite of mine. I cook this as often as I can purchase a chaudin. During the harvest crew meals, all the men look forward to partaking of this special dish. I never stuff it anymore as these are available in groceries already stuffed. But I still have the recipe.

1   **medium size chaudin (hog's stomach)**
1   **6 ounce box baking soda**
½   **cup vinegar**
2   **quarts water**
4   **pounds pork, ground coarsely**
1½   **cup chopped onion**
1   **cup chopped parsley**
1   **cup green onion tops, chopped**
3   **cloves minced garlic**
    salt and pepper to taste
⅔   **cup water**

Clean out all debris out of chaudin. Soak in soda water for a couple of hours. Scrape out outer surface real well. Rinse well in vinegar water (½ cup vinegar and 1 quart water) making sure the inside is real clean. Allow to dry. Set aside.

Combine pork, onion, parsley and garlic in large bowl. Add salt and pepper as desired. Stuff the meat mixture firmly into chaudin. Close cavity, securing real well by sewing with a large sewing needle and thread. You may also use toothpicks to secure the cavity if necessary. Spray a heavy roaster with PAM. Line the bottom with oil. Lay the chaudin in the bottom. Sprinkle with salt and pepper and paprika. Puncture the chaudin with a large meat fork in several places to prevent rupturing, place in oven carefully and allow to brown on broil on both sides for another 15-20 minutes, basting occasionally. Turn temperature to 350 degrees and bake for 2 hours basting occasionally. Turn over twice during the baking. Slice and serve on platter. Ladle gravy over chaudin to keep moist and enhance the taste. Serves 6.

Kraut Special

3   **pounds pork meat (I use pork chops)**
1   **2 pound jar of sauerkraut (I prefer the jars)**
3   **medium potatoes, cubed**
    water to boil sauerkraut and pork
    salt and pepper

Put pork in a large pot. Add enough water to cover meat plus 2 inches over the meat. Boil until tender. Save stock. In another large pot put sauerkraut, which has been drained and rinsed with cold water, and enough water to boil sauerkraut for 2 hours. As you boil the kraut, add potatoes and continue to boil. You may need to add more water to sauerkraut, use as much of the pork stock as possible. After boiling sauerkraut for a couple of hours, put the pork into the sauerkraut pot. Season and continue cooking on medium heat for 30 more minutes. Serve with or without rice. Serves 2-3.

Rinse sauerkraut as much as possible as this makes it taste better.

This recipe is in honor of my husband, The General (this title was given to him by Mr. Lonnie Walters on a pleasure trip up the Rhine River). This is his favorite meal even though I seldom cook it. I just cannot tolerate the smell of sauerkraut. Harry, The General, was real happy when his mother gave me the recipe. I can't prepare it as well as she can. Maybe it is because I simply do not like the taste.

NOTES

POULTRY

By the look on the face of the chicken on the opposite page, it seems like that chicken's days are numbered. Chicken gumbo, sauce piquant, dumplings, fricassee and chicken stew are just a few of the many Cajun dishes that are favorites.

Of course, every home had a chicken yard. Usually, the Cajun alarm clock was the rooster crowing in the yard. One of the chores that the Cajun children have is to pick the eggs out of the nests.

POULTRY

Cajun Chicken & Dumplings

This dish I especially enjoyed when my mother cooked it. Her dumplings were always perfect. My husband doesn't care for dumplings, but to me, there is no better way to cook chicken.

1　hen, cut up
2　cups cooking oil
2　cups chopped onions
1　cup chopped bell pepper
1　pint water
　　salt and pepper to taste
　　dumplings

Brown hen in oil. Remove chicken pieces and add onions and bell pepper and sauté. Remove excess oil. Put chicken back in pot and add water. Season well with salt and pepper. Cover and simmer until meat is tender. Add more water if necessary. Drop dumplings in gravy, cover tightly and cook for 15 minutes (do not raise cover while cooking as the dumplings will not steam well and fall apart).

Dumplings

2　cups sifted flour
1　teaspoon salt
½　teaspoon baking powder
¼　teaspoon baking soda
1　beaten egg
⅔　cup milk, approximately
2　tablespoons melted butter
¼　cup chopped green onion tops

Sift together all dry ingredients. Add egg, butter, green onion tops, and enough milk to make a stiff batter. Drop by tablespoons into gravy. Cover and allow to cook for 15 minutes. Serve over rice. Serves 6

Chicken Sauce Piquant

1   hen or large fryer
    salt and pepper to taste
2   cups oil
1   cup chopped onions
1   cup chopped bell pepper
½   cup chopped celery
1   large can stewed tomatoes
1   small can tomato sauce or 3 cups
    tomato juice
2   tablespoons roux
1   quart water

This is also a good harvest crew meal. The more of this in a pot, the better it tastes. This dish was served on request to our good friend, Mr. Freddie Strange from Wimmer. This is truly an old Cajun recipe. The fresh tomato juice is best to use if available. If the gravy is too thin, you can always thicken it with the old standby, cornstarch.

Brown seasoned hen or fryer in hot oil. Remove chicken pieces. Add onions, bell pepper, celery, and sauté. Remove as much oil as possible. Add stewed tomatoes and tomato sauce or juice. Bring to a boil. Add roux. Stir until roux is blended well. Add chicken pieces and cook on high heat until chicken is tender and done (about 1 hour). Add water in small amounts if the gravy gets too thick before the meat is done. Serve over rice. Serves 4-6.

Cornichon (page 93) is excellent with this dish.

Fried Chicken à Chin

This is how my mother used to fry chicken. Quite different from how I fry it now. But none the less, either way is great!

1 **fryer, cut up into serving pieces**
   salt and pepper to taste
3 **cups yellow corn meal**
   oil for deep frying

Wash and cut up fryer. Season, then roll in corn meal until well coated. Drop in hot oil in a frying skillet, covering at least half of the fryer pieces. Fry until golden brown on both sides. Do not turn over too often. About 10 minutes on each side is all that is necessary if the fryer is not too large. Serves 3.

Mine

1 **fryer, cut up into serving pieces**
   salt and pepper to taste
2 **eggs, beaten**
2-3 **cups flour**
   oil for deep frying in heavy pot

Wash and cut up fryer. Season. Run through eggs. Dredge through flour until well coated. Drop in hot oil and allow to fry to a golden brown on one side before turning over. Fry to a golden brown on that side. It may be necessary to turn over once more to complete cooking. Remove from grease and lay on platter that has been lined with absorbent towels. Serves 3.

Chicken Gumbo

1 **cup flour**
1 **cup oil**
 hen or fryer, cut into serving pieces
1 **gallon water**
 salt and pepper to taste
1 **cup chopped onion**
½ **cup chopped bell pepper**
¼ **cup chopped celery**
1 **pound sausage-optional**
¼ **cup onion tops**

This is my favorite gumbo. My mother always used a fresh hen and that made it even better. I remember her catching a hen and ringing its neck in order to kill it. It would jump all over the yard. That was the funniest sight I have ever seen. Now, I always go to the store and purchase a hen or a fryer. Takes all the fun out of it but the taste is still there.

Make a dark roux with flour and oil. Add water slowly and allow to boil on medium high. Add hen or fryer and season to taste. Add onion, bell pepper, and celery and continue to boil until meat is tender. If a large hen is used, boil for at least 2 hours. If a fryer is used, boil only 1 hour. If you are using sliced smoked sausage, you have to add the sausage to the pot when you add the meat. This does add a special flavor to the gumbo. Finally, add the chopped green onions and boil for 10 more minutes. Serve in gumbo bowl over rice. Serves 4-6.

NOTES

Krispy Chicken à Linda

This is one of the many dishes which we prepare for our harvest crew meals. It is easy to fix for 20-25 men at noon, and that is what we look for - an easy, simple dish that tastes good and is also nutritional.

1 3-pound fryer, cut into serving pieces
1 stick of melted margarine
1 medium size box Rice Krispies cereal
    salt and pepper to taste

Spray pan with PAM and layer with half the Rice Krispies and seasoned chicken, skin side up. Pour melted margarine over chicken. Cover with remaining Rice Krispies. Put loose sheet of foil over pan while baking at 375 degrees for 1 hour 20 minutes. Do not cover tightly. Serves 4.

Baked Chicken or Cornish Hen

This can be served anytime to anyone and it is a hit. I cook this at least once a week. I usually serve rice dressing or wild rice to accompany it.

1 large fryer or 2 cornish hens
    salt and pepper to taste
½ cup water

Wash chicken or hens, season with salt and pepper. Spray a baking dish with PAM and lay the fowl breast side up on bottom of pan. Bake in oven at 400 degrees for one hour, basting occasionally with gravy that forms from fowl. Turn fowl over on the other side and allow to brown, this takes about 20-25 more minutes. Remove and carve. While carving, add ½ cup water to bottom of pan and form a gravy by scratching the bottom. Serve fowl and gravy together over rice. Serves 3-4.

Chicken Fricassee

1 hen, cup into pieces
1 cup butter or oil
1 cup chopped onion
1 cup chopped bell pepper
½ cup chopped celery
½ cup chopped onion tops
½ cup chopped parsley
4 small smoked ham hocks
3 cups ground chicken gizzards (2 pounds)
   water (approximately 2½ pints)
   salt and pepper to taste

Recently, at a camp supper, a cousin, Steve Zaunbrecher, reminded me of an old Cajun dish, Chicken Fricassee. I enjoyed visiting with our cousins and I thoroughly enjoyed the meal.

Season the hen pieces. Brown the hen in oil until golden brown. Remove hen pieces and set aside. Add chopped onion, bell pepper and celery to the pot and brown well. Add ham hocks and chicken and about 1 pint of water. Continue cooking on medium high heat until the hen is real tender. This may take a couple of hours, depending on how tough the hen is. While this is being done, cook the ground chicken gizzards in a separate pot that has been sprayed with PAM. Cook slowly as not to burn, adding dabs of water to brown. When all is finished cooking, add the ground cooked gizzards to the pot of chicken and add chopped onion tops and parsley. If there is not enough gravy in the pot, add about ½ pint of water until a gravy is formed. Mix well and serve over rice. Serves 4-6.

Fryers can be used to shorten the cooking time. The ground raw gizzards can also be added to the chicken pot after the chicken has been browned.

The Duck Hunt

No one can properly describe the beauty of a duck hunt. But let me try —We get up at 5 o'clock in the morning, drink a pot of coffee as we dress for the hunt. I put on my long johns, thermal socks and my camouflage suit. By the way, it had better be waterproof and warm! Then I slip on these long rubber boots called waders. And if I'm lucky enough to still be able to walk, I will grab my 12 guage shot gun on my way out to the duck blind.

The trip to the blind is about a mile out in a rice field that is flooded with water to attract the ducks. Luckily, we travel by four-wheeled motor bikes (camouflaged, of course).

One of the hunters is usually a designated duck caller. So his job is to lure the ducks close enough for us to shoot. In doing so, we usually get our limit for the day. If we are lucky, our black Labrador retriever (dog) will go get all our ducks and bring them back to us.

Then we return home to eat a hearty breakfast and to clean our ducks. A good duck gumbo or pot roasted ducks are in store for tonight. The performance is repeated every morning during the duck hunting season.

DUCK

Duck or Goose Gumbo à Gueydan

This was and still is a favorite during winter. Ducks and geese were always plentiful in South Louisiana, so we learned many ways to prepare them . Of course, Cajuns make gumbo with anything they could because it's the most popular dish among us and others.

2   ducks or one goose, cut into sections
    salt and pepper to taste
1   pound smoked sausage
1   cup oil
1   cup flour
1   gallon water
1   cup chopped onion
¾   cup chopped green onion tops
¾   cup chopped bell pepper

Dress goose or ducks by washing well. Cut into serving-size pieces and season with salt and pepper. Cut up sausage into inch-long links. Set aside. Brown flour and oil to make a dark roux. Add water slowly and bring to a boil. Add game and sausage to roux mixture and add onions, bell peppers and green onion tops. Continue to medium boil for about 2 hours or until game is tender. The older and larger the game is, the longer it will take to cook. The amount of water you use depends on how much gumbo juice you wish to have. Serve over rice. Serves 4-6.

Pot Roasted Duck Gueydan

2 **ducks, cleaned**
1 **medium onion, halved**
1 **small bell pepper, sliced**
2 **slices bacon**
1 **small red potato, quartered**
salt and pepper to taste
¾ **cup oil**
2 **cups water**

Prepare ducks. Season with salt and pepper. In cavity, stuff half of onion, half of bell pepper and half of potato in each duck. Sew cavity closed with a large sewing needle and sewing thread. Add to hot oil in deep heavy pot. Brown well on all sides over a medium heat. As you brown, you may need to add dabs of water. Cover after each browning, continue to turn over and over and add water until ducks are tender. This usually takes about 2½ hours, depending on how tough the ducks are. Carve ducks on platter. Then add a small amount of water to the bottom of the pot to form a gravy. Serve over rice. Serves 4.

Wild ducks were always plentiful in South Louisiana. My father used to bring home 20-30 ducks for my mother to clean. That was a horrible job. Thank God that the men now kill and clean or have cleaned their game before bringing them home for the wives to prepare. I can remember helping to clean ducks as a young girl. My job was to "PICK" them (pull feathers off) and my mother gutted them. As hard as this was, we really enjoyed sitting down at the table once my mother cooked them, but not until the next day.

Duck & Dressing à Vincent

This is a follow up to the duck on the preceding page. My brother-in-law taught me to do this. That makes us both older and wiser.

½ **cup chopped onion**
¼ **cup chopped bell pepper**
¼ **cup chopped celery**
1 **pound ground beef**
3 **cups cooked rice**
¼ **cup chopped green onions**

Once the ducks are fully cooked, remove them from the pot. To the already formed gravy, add onion, bell pepper and celery. Sauté. Add ground beef and cook until thoroughly done on medium heat about 20 minutes. Add cooked rice and green onions. Salt and pepper to taste and mix thoroughly. Lay ducks on top of dressing, cover and simmer for 10 minutes on low heat. Remove ducks and carve on platter. Serve with dressing. Serves 4-6.

Notes

CRAWFISH

Each spring thoughts of crawfish fill the heads of most people in South Louisiana. As the leaves burst out and the warm breezes fan the country side, speculation grows about how these small crustaceans have fared through the winter. Groups of bayou dwellers huddle about the water's edge in ever more earnest conversation about the extent of the spring runoff, prices of the previous seasons and the quality of the meat. Mostly they talk about price.

Louisiana is said to produce 99 percent of this country's crawfish harvest, an amount which may be anything from 6 to 20 million pounds, depending on climatic conditions. About 88 percent of the total stays right there in south Louisiana. The rest is shipped to other areas and states.

It is common to see boats going through flooded fields gathering crawfish from submerged cages. Ideally, these boats are manned by two men, one for driving and the other for pulling up the nets and emptying the crawfish on board into sacks. This is very hard and tedious work.

Rice and soybean farmers often harvest crawfish from their flooded fields before planting their annual crop, thus earning a second income from the land.

These small crustaceans used to grow wild in Louisiana. However, a very unique way of farming has derived from a market that is much in demand because of the many delicious dishes which are now enjoyed not only by Cajuns but by people all over the world.

CRAWFISH

Boiled Crawfish

You have never really lived until you have gone to a crawfish boil. Imagine sitting around a big, long table surrounded by friends and relatives and gobs of big, red, luscious crawfish. It is what a Cajun calls a celebration that cannot be described in a dictionary. Don't forget to cover your table with newspaper. Make sure you have plenty of large trays to hold the boiled crawfish and the shells. Most of all, have plenty of absorbent paper towels on hand. This is a deliciously messy meal.

6 **gallons or more boiling water**
1 **large onion, cut in quarters**
2 **lemons, cut in half**
6-8 **unpeeled potatoes**
6 **shucked and cleaned ears of corn**
3 **ounces liquid crab boil**
plenty of salt & pepper
25 **pounds of crawfish**

Bring water to a boil in a large 10-15 gallon pot. Add lemon, onions, potatoes and corn. Bring all ingredients to a hard boil. Add 25 pounds of crawfish, which have been rinsed with cold water until they are clean. Add the crab boil and bring to a hard boil again. Cover and boil for 7-10 minutes. Remove crawfish and spread on the table covered with newspaper or in large ice chests. Sprinkle a lot of salt & pepper over the boiled crawfish. Serves 3-4

Do not season with salt while boiling because this makes the crawfish shells hard to peel. To peel, pull the tails away from the bodies and peel as you do shrimp. Serve hot with cold drinks.

Crawfish Party Mold

3   **envelopes of plain gelatin**
½   **cup hot water**
3   **pounds crawfish tails, chopped coarsely**
1   **10 ounce can of tomato soup**
1   **8 ounce package of cream cheese**
½   **cup finely chopped onion**
½   **cup finely chopped celery**
1   **cup mayonnaise**
1   **teaspoon baking soda**

Whenever I prepare foods for a wedding or a party, I always insist on doing this mold. It can be used as a centerpiece, to be eaten, or put in a different mold as a dip with fancy crackers. I always get a lot of comments on this monster of a crawfish. A friend of mine, Erma Jean Miller from Eunice, introduced me to this gorgeous creature.

Dissolve gelatin in luke warm water. Heat soup and add crawfish. Cook for 20 minutes on medium heat. Stir often to prevent sticking. Add cream cheese, onions and celery. Cook until cheese is melted. Add gelatin and mayonnaise and stir until well blended. Remove from heat. Add baking soda and stir quickly while mixture foams. Prepare the molds by coating with extra mayonnaise or spraying with PAM. Pour the mixture directly into molds. Allow to set overnight. Garnish. Yields 6 cups. This is always a hit.

NOTES

Mama's Crawfish Bisque

My father-in-law did not eat crawfish until my mother cooked this dish for him. Then after that, he could not eat enough of crawfish. I guess my grandmother taught her all she knew about cooking, so that is where she learned to prepare this dish. And I guess I learned it from her. It is very rich and very, very good.

30	pounds whole, fresh crawfish
	water, enough to cover the crawfish bodies
60-70	cleaned shells
2	pounds of peeled tail meat of the crawfish
1	whole medium head of garlic, peeled and ground
1	cup ground bell pepper
1	cup ground onion
10	slices of bread, ground
	salt and pepper to taste
2	cups flour
2	cups oil
2	quarts water
2	pounds peeled crawfish tails
1	cup chopped green onions
	Louisiana Red Hot Sauce to taste

To prepare crawfish, scald whole crawfish in a large pot of boiling water for 5 minutes. Pull tails away from bodies. Peel tails and put meat aside. To clean the bodies that have been scalded, use a pineapple spoon or one that has a serrated edge, and scoop out the insides, cleaning shell well of debris, remove eyes and feelers. Rinse thoroughly. Set aside.

To prepare stuffing, grind 2 pounds tail meat coarsely with onions, bell peppers, and garlic. Add seasoning, salt and pepper to taste. Mix thoroughly. Add ground bread slices to crawfish mixture and mix thoroughly until firm in consistency (form small balls in palm of hand).

To stuff shells, take 1½ teaspoon of stuffing and pack firmly into body shells until all the stuffing has been used. Set aside and allow to set in

Continued on next page

refrigerator over night if possible.

To prepare the gravy, mix oil and flour in a heavy 4 quart saucepan. Cook over a medium high heat,stirring constantly until dark brown. Add 1 quart water slowly and allow to slow boil for 30 minutes until pretty thick. You can add more water if necessary to make gravy lighter, do not exceed one quart.

To prepare the finished product, add the stuffed crawfish bodies to the roux gravy which is slowly boiling. Then add the rest of the whole crawfish tails. Add the onion tops and season to taste with salt, pepper and Louisiana Red Hot Sauce. Allow to cook on a medium heat for thirty minutes. Serve in gumbo bowl over rice. Serves 8-10.

This dish is time-consuming but it is worth it. I usually take two days to prepare it.

NOTES

Crawfish Etouffee

I have already cooked this for the entire Zaunbrecher family in Jones. My father-in-law would bring fresh crawfish tails and we would enjoy a big family get-together. It is also one of my specialties. I do not know how I managed to formulate this dish, I just know that this is how I have always cooked it. Use fresh crawfish or tail meat that has not been frozen long. The fat of crawfish frozen for a long period of time may get rancid (stale) and that would ruin the etouffee. If it is frozen for a while, simply thaw and run cold water over the tails to rinse off the fat before putting into gravy.

½ cup flour
1 cup oil
¾ cup onions, chopped
½ bell pepper, chopped
¼ cup celery, chopped
1½ pints water
2 pounds crawfish tails
salt and pepper to taste
½ cup chopped green onion tops
¼ cup chopped parsley

Make a light roux. Add onions, bell pepper and celery. Sauté until limp and shiny. Add water and bring to a medium boil. Slow boil for 30 minutes. Add crawfish tails, salt, pepper, onion tops and parsley. Stir well. Allow to slow boil for 20 minutes. Serve over rice. Serves 4-5.

Crawfish & Shrimp Jambalaya

1	pound smoked sausage or andouille
½	cup oil
1	cup onion, chopped
¾	bell pepper, chopped
¼	cup celery, chopped
1	8 ounce can tomato sauce
1	cup green onions, chopped
	salt & pepper to taste
2	cups rice, uncooked
4	cups water
1	pound crawfish tails
1	pound shrimp, peeled

This is one that is hard to beat. Mixing the two most popular seafoods together brings double pleasure to the taste buds! We cooked this on a weekly basis at home whenever the fresh seafood was in season. Sometimes, my mother would use dried shrimp, boiled and peeled (about an ounce) to give it that extra special flavor.

Slice sausage or andouille thinly and fry in oil. Remove from pot and drain on paper towel. Add the onion, celery, bell pepper and sauté in the oil left in the pot. Add the tomato sauce and season to taste. Slow cook for 30 minutes. Add the rice, green onion, water, and shrimp and crawfish and sausage. Bring it all to a boil. When the rice has almost absorbed all the water, stir well with a fork, cover and allow to simmer for 15 minutes.

If you are making only shrimp jambalaya, use 2 pounds shrimp; if you are making only crawfish jambalaya, use 2 pounds crawfish. Serve with a salad for a complete meal. Serves 8.

Fried Crawfish Tails

oil to deep fat fry
2 **eggs, beaten**
1 **pound crawfish tails**
 salt & pepper to taste
2 **cups flour**

While oil is heating in a deep fat fryer, or a deep heavy pot, beat eggs well. Add crawfish tail meat and coat well with egg. Then roll tails in seasoned flour. (I usually put the flour in a small paper sack and shake the tails real well-this coats them evenly with much less trouble and mess.) Drop coated tails in hot oil, 400 degrees, and fry until golden brown, about 3-5 minutes. Drain on paper towel and serve hot. Large tails are always better than smaller ones as you can taste the flavor of the crawfish more than just the batter which happens when small tails are used. Serves 3-4

Crawfish Gumbo

1 **cup oil**
1 **cup flour**
2 **quarts water**
2 **pounds crawfish tails**
salt & pepper to taste
1 **cup green onion, chopped**

Make roux dark brown by using flour and oil. Add water slowly. Allow to slow boil for about 30 minutes. Add crawfish tails, seasoning and onion tops. Cook on medium heat for 20 more minutes. Serve over rice. Serves 4.

Shrimp may be used as a substitute for crawfish.

We have so many different types of gumbos. Cajuns always cook gumbo with special meals or just make special meals out of a gumbo. That is another dish that is as good or even better the day after it has been cooked. A good hot plate (bowl) of gumbo on a cold winter night just cannot be expressed with words, English words that is. A small bowl of potato salad always accompanies the gumbo.

NOTES

Crawfish Pie

Actually, I have never made this for my family. However, a wedding, or any social affair is not complete without this dish. It truly deserves to be mentioned in an old Cajun's favorite song.

Roux

1 **cup oil or butter**
1 **cup flour**

Cook the above, stirring constantly until it reaches a light brown color. Set aside.

2 **cups chopped onions**
1 **cup chopped green bell pepper**
1 **cup chopped celery**
2 **pounds chopped crawfish tail meat**
¼ **cup chopped green onion tops**
¼ **cup chopped fresh parsley**
salt and pepper to taste
4 **cups water (approximately)**
¼ **cup white wine**
2 **tablespoons cornstarch**
2 **cups cooked, cooled rice**

To the roux, add onions, bell pepper and celery. Cook until limp. Add water slowly to mixture, stirring well, and slow boil for 10 minutes. Add crawfish tail meat, green onions and parsley. Season to taste and cook on medium heat for 20 minutes. Stir in cornstarch which has been dissolved in wine. Add rice and mix thoroughly. Pour into unbaked pie shell and bake at 350 degrees for 20-30 minutes or until golden brown, or pour into basic tart shell (see facing page) and serve hot.

Basic Tart Shell

- 3 **cups flour**
- 1½ **teaspoon salt**
- 1 **cup shortening**
- 5-6 **tablespoon cold water**

Combine salt and flour in bowl. Cut in shortening with a pastry blender until it resembles coarse meal. Sprinkle water evenly over dough and stir with a fork until all dry ingredients are moistened. Shape dough into a ball. Chill. On a lightly floured board, roll dough to ⅛ inch thickness. Cut with a 2 inch cutter in a round circle. Fit each pastry tart shell into a miniature muffin pan and prick each tart with a fork. Bake in 400 degrees oven for 10 minutes or until golden brown. Makes about 8 dozen tart shells.

NOTES

Cena Mae's Crawfish Egg Rolls

This recipe only recently caught my attention. My sister-in-law, Cena Mae, had served it for her harvest crew meals and my husband really enjoyed it. So now it is a regular for us.

1 cup chopped onions
1 cup chopped bell pepper
1 cup chopped celery
2 sticks margarine
¼ cup parsley
2 cans cream of mushroom soup
1 small jar Pace picante sauce
2 pounds crawfish tails
2 cups cooked rice
 salt and pepper to taste
1 large package egg roll wrappers
 oil for deep frying

Sauté onion, bell pepper and celery in margarine. Add parsley, picante sauce and cream of mushroom soup. Mix well. Add crawfish and cooked rice. Season to taste and bake in 325 degree oven for 30 minutes. Roll ingredients in wrappers as directed by package. Deep fry for 3-4 minutes or until golden brown. This may be prepared and frozen for 1 month. Excellent as an etouffee or casserole.

NOTES

Nunney's Crawfish Au Gratin

½   pound margarine
1   cup diced onions
¼   cup diced celery
4   tablespoon flour
1   large can Carnation milk
1   10 ounce package Velveeta cheese
2   egg yolks, beaten
2   pounds crawfish tails

Sauté onions and celery. Mix flour and Carnation milk in a bowl. Pour into sautéed mixture and stir well. Cook on medium heat until thickened. Add cheese, reserving ¼ of package for topping. When completely melted, add egg yolks and mix well. Add crawfish and cook for 15 minutes on low heat, stirring often. Pour into a greased casserole dish. Add cheese for topping and bake at 375 degrees until cheese melts, about 15 minutes.

This sister-in-law will always be special to me because I could not have dated my husband if it wouldn't have been for her. My parents did not allow me to date anyone without a suitable chaperone. She was my husband's younger sister so poor Ramona (Nunney) had to come along every time we went out on a date. She never seemed to mind and we always all had a good time. We do share a lot of caring between us. After she got married, and my husband returned from serving 18 months in Berlin, Germany in the Army, things were not the same. So we simply got married.

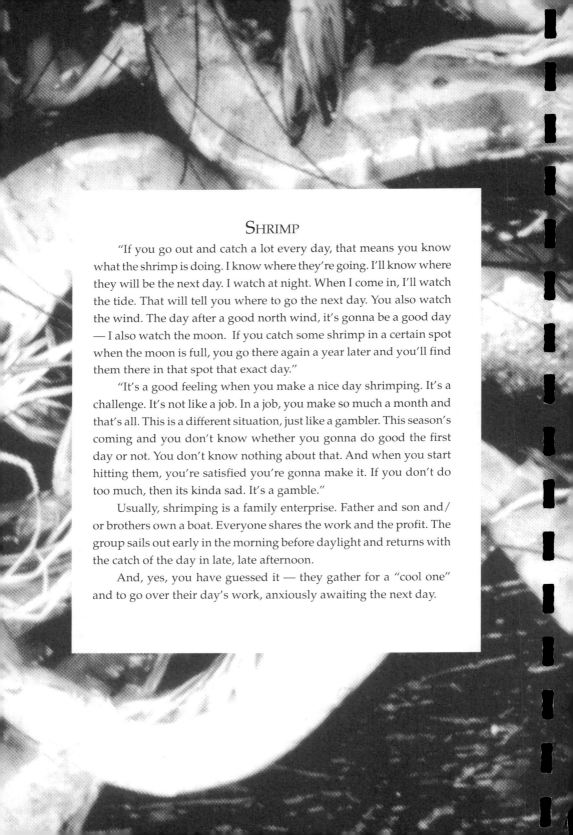

SHRIMP

"If you go out and catch a lot every day, that means you know what the shrimp is doing. I know where they're going. I'll know where they will be the next day. I watch at night. When I come in, I'll watch the tide. That will tell you where to go the next day. You also watch the wind. The day after a good north wind, it's gonna be a good day — I also watch the moon. If you catch some shrimp in a certain spot when the moon is full, you go there again a year later and you'll find them there in that spot that exact day."

"It's a good feeling when you make a nice day shrimping. It's a challenge. It's not like a job. In a job, you make so much a month and that's all. This is a different situation, just like a gambler. This season's coming and you don't know whether you gonna do good the first day or not. You don't know nothing about that. And when you start hitting them, you're satisfied you're gonna make it. If you don't do too much, then its kinda sad. It's a gamble."

Usually, shrimping is a family enterprise. Father and son and/ or brothers own a boat. Everyone shares the work and the profit. The group sails out early in the morning before daylight and returns with the catch of the day in late, late afternoon.

And, yes, you have guessed it — they gather for a "cool one" and to go over their day's work, anxiously awaiting the next day.

SHRIMP

Shrimp-Eggplant Casserole

Eggplant complements shrimp very well. So, when we got tired of eating fried shrimp or shrimp gumbo, Mama always served this together. She, however, cooked hers in a pot on top of the stove. Somehow, the casserole crept into the scene.

2 medium eggplants, peeled and diced
1 cup onion, finely chopped
¼ cup celery, finely chopped
½ cup bell pepper, finely chopped
½ pound butter or margarine, melted
½ cup bread crumbs
   salt & pepper to taste
2 pounds of fresh shrimp, peeled

Sauté but do not brown the eggplant, onion, bell pepper and celery in butter. Cook on low fire for one hour. Add shrimp and cook for 10 minutes. Add seasoning and bread crumbs and then pour into a large casserole dish that has been sprayed with Pam, or pour into individual dishes. Bake at 350 degrees until slightly browned-about 20 minutes.

This is delicious. If you can, scoop out the eggplant and use the shell to bake in. Bell peppers can also be cored out and used. Just stuff them and bake as you would a casserole. Serves 6.

NOTES

Fried Shrimp

2 **pounds fresh shrimp, peeled and deveined**
3 **eggs, beaten**
3 **cups flour**
  salt & pepper to taste
  oil for deep fat frying

Dip shrimp into eggs. Dredge into flour which has been highly seasoned and coat well. Drop into hot oil and fry for 3-5 minutes, or until golden brown. Serves 4-5.

I cannot get enough of this dish and once you have eaten this, you will never want shrimp prepared any other way. When we eat this at home, I prepare some French fries but I never get around to eating the fries—I wonder why?

Shrimp Sauce Piquant

1 **pint water**
2 **tablespoons of roux**
1 **14 ounce can of tomato sauce**
1 **6 ounce can tomato paste**
½ **cup onion, chopped**
½ **cup bell pepper, chopped**
¼ **cup celery, chopped**
3 **pounds shrimp, peeled**
  salt & pepper to taste

Bring one pint of water to a boil. Add roux, tomato sauce and tomato paste. Stir until blended. Add onion, bell pepper, celery and cook for 1 hour on medium boil. Add shrimp and cook for 30 minutes. If thick, add a small amount of water to form required thickness. Season to taste. Serve over rice.

Any type of fish can also be used in this dish, even turtle or alligator. Simply add turtle meat, fish, or alligator meat instead of shrimp. Cook for 1 hour longer on medium boil or until meat is tender. Serves 8.

Piquants were a family favorite to serve for friends. The piquant gravy would cook slowly while family and friends played a good game of cards usually Rook or Booray. Money was never exchanged, they used beans or matches to make their bets with. I always stood behind Mama or another lady and helped them to play. I do not play cards anymore, but I still remember the good times I had.

Shrimp-Okra Gumbo

This is another one of my favorites that my father-in-law taught me how to make. He used to brew a large pot full of shrimp-okra gumbo, and all the family would come over—one great thing about gumbo is that you can always add more water to accommodate the number of unexpected guests. My husband is not too fond of okra, but once in while I treat myself to this dish.

4	cups okra, freshly cut or frozen
½	cup oil
¾	cup flour
¾	cup oil
1	cup onion, chopped
¾	cup bell pepper, chopped
¼	cup celery, chopped
4	quarts water
	salt & pepper to taste
2	pounds shrimp, peeled
½	cup green onion, chopped

Smother okra in oil for about 20 minutes on medium heat, stirring constantly not to burn. In a large pot, make a roux by browning the flour and oil until they reach a medium brown color. Add onion, bell pepper, and celery and sauté until they wilt. Add okra and water and season with salt and pepper. Cook on medium heat for 1 hour. Add shrimp and green onion tops. Cook for 20 minutes at medium boil. Serve over rice. Serves 6.

NOTES

Fried Shrimp à Chin

1 **pound shrimp, peeled and deveined**
2 **cups yellow corn meal**
   oil for deep frying
   salt and pepper to taste

Roll shrimp in corn meal and coat well. Drop in hot oil and deep fry until golden brown. (About 5 minutes.) Drain on paper towels placed in a platter. Season with salt and pepper to taste. Serves 2.

This is another style of frying that my mother did that I have learned to do differently. Not because I did not like the way she did it but because we need variations at times. Cajuns do a lot of fried foods but never are their foods greasy. They are always fried very crisp with no oil residue on the foods.

Shrimp Casserole

1 **pound peeled shrimp**
¼ **cup margarine**
½ **cup chopped onion**
½ **cup chopped green pepper**
½ **cup chopped celery**
¼ **cup margarine**
1 **10¾ ounce can Cream of Mushroom soup**
½ **10¾ ounce can Cheddar Cheese soup**
2½ **cups cooked long grain rice**
½ **cup green onions**

Sauté shrimp in margarine. Sauté onion, green pepper and celery in margarine. Add Cream of Mushroom soup, Cheddar Cheese soup and shrimp. Mix. Add rice and green onions. Mix thoroughly. Pour into 9x13 inch casserole pan that has been sprayed with PAM. Bake at 350 degrees for 30-40 minutes. Serves 8.

I do not make casseroles often, but this one is the one that I always make for special company. It is so easy and can be prepared beforehand. Simply refrigerate or freeze until you are ready to cook. As a matter of fact, it is even better if it is made the day before serving. Always bake to serve hot.

Shrimp Stew

¾ cup flour
¾ cup oil
1 quart water
½ cup chopped onions
¼ cup chopped bell pepper
2 pounds peeled shrimp
   salt and pepper to taste
¼ cup chopped green onions

Brown flour to make roux. Gradually add water, then add onions and bell pepper. Allow to slow boil for 30 minutes. The gravy should be thick. Add shrimp, salt and pepper and chopped green onion tops. Medium boil for 20 minutes. Turn off heat and serve. Serves 4-6.

Shrimp & Crab Cornbread Dressing

1 nine-inch cornbread
½ cup chopped onions
3 tablespoons oil
1 cup jalapeno cheese, grated
1 16 ounce can creamed corn
1 1 cup chopped shrimp
1 cup crab meat
   salt and pepper

Prepare cornbread. Set aside. Brown onions in oil. Add shrimp and crab and sauté. Add creamed corn and cook for 10 minutes. Crumble cornbread well into seafood mixture. Blend well. Season to taste. Pour into baking dish that has been sprayed with PAM. Sprinkle with cheese. Bake at 350 degrees for 20 minutes. Serves 4-6.

Shrimp Gumbo

  1 **cup flour**
  1 **cup oil**
  2 **quarts water**
  2 **pounds shrimp**
1½ **cups chopped green onions**
  6 **hard-boiled eggs**

Brown flour and oil to make a dark roux. Slowly add water and allow to medium boil for 30 minutes. Add shrimp and green onions. Slow boil for 20 minutes. Add boiled eggs, cutting 3 in half and putting the other 3 in whole and cook for 10 minutes on medium boil. Serve over rice. Serves 4.

You can make a big seafood gumbo by omitting the eggs and having all of the above plus 1 pound of crab meat and 1 pint of oysters, juice included, and slow boil for 20 minutes. That's what I call a meal fit for a king and his majesties.

When I think of seafood. I think of shrimp gumbo because it is easy to purchase and prepare. You can bet your life that when the first cool spell arrives, I will be preparing shrimp gumbo for supper at my house. My mother always put boiled eggs in our shrimp gumbo. It really added to the flavor even though not many people have ever heard of it.

NOTES

OYSTERS

At the courthouse, they told me all the old tax rolls and steamboat records had been destroyed by a fire in 1885, and so here I sit in a quaint little oyster house off Magdalene Square, consoling myself with the tender companionship of the succulent bivalve on the half-shell.

M. DuPuy, proprietor of this popular resort, tells me the oysters he and his assistant are shucking for me and these other hungry Acadians are of his own cultivation, reared in his own oyster beds with the same loving care that a Texas rancher feels for his dogies.

Never have I tasted more delicious fat oysters, and the price is ridiculous: 60 cents a dozen!

While I finished my first dozen, the gentlemen at the next table put away four dozen and was now at work on his fifth.

"Alors, madame," I asked Mme. DuPuy, wife of the proprietor, who works as a waitress. "What is the greatest number of oysters you have ever seen a gentleman consume at a sitting?"

"Twenty-four dozen," she replied. "But he was faster than you."

"A gentleman from Texas, no doubt," I suggested.

"Non, monsieur. He was M. Bertram from Kaplan."

(Story courtesy of DuPuy's Oyster House in Abbeville, La.)

OYSTERS

Seafood Cornbread Dressing

1   9-inch pan of cornbread
½   cup chopped onions
3   tablespoons oil
½   cup chopped celery
½   cup chopped parsley
½   cup chopped green onions
1   cup grated jalapeno cheese
1   can cream of shrimp soup
1   cup chopped shrimp
1   cup oysters, drained
1   cup crab meat
    salt and pepper to taste

Prepare cornbread and set aside. In a medium saucepan, brown onions. Add celery, parsley, and green onion tops and cook for 5 minutes on medium high heat. Add cream of shrimp soup (diluted with water), shrimp, oysters, and crab meat. Season to taste. Bring to a boil on medium heat (about 15 minutes). Crumble cornbread into seafood mixture. Blend well. Add cheese and stir. Pour into casserole sprayed with PAM. Bake at 350 degrees for 15 minutes. Serves 6.

Fried Oysters à Chin

1 **pint oysters, drained**
2 **cups yellow corn meal**
   oil for deep frying
   salt and pepper

Roll oysters in corn meal. Drop immediately in hot oil and deep fry until golden brown.(I like mine very crisp.) Season with salt and pepper to taste. Serves 2

Oysters are delicious any way you cook them. But I really prefer them raw. However, we always fried our oysters because my father just could not swallow a raw oyster. Mama never seasoned the oysters before cooking them and I do not season them until after they are fried to a crisp golden brown. This is the way Mama fried them and I do the very same.

NOTES

Oyster Rice Dressing

Every holiday, we had baked turkey. And, of course, my mother always stuffed the turkey with this dressing. It was an old family tradition. The dressing was often tastier than the main dish. I can still visualize Mama sewing up the turkey's cavity that she had stuffed to capacity. Then she baked it making sure none of it escaped until it was ready to be served.

¼ **cup oil**
   giblets from fowl, chopped
1 **cup chopped onion**
½ **cup chopped bell pepper**
¼ **cup chopped celery**
1 **pint oysters, undrained**
3 **cups cooked rice**
½ **cup chopped onion tops**
¼ **cup chopped parsley**
   salt and pepper

Brown chopped giblets in oil until brown, add chopped onions, bell pepper and celery. Cook with giblets on medium heat until light brown. Add oysters and juice and cook for about 10 minutes. Add onion tops, parsley and rice. Season well. Mix all together. Stuff fowl (hen, fryer or turkey) with enough mixture to fill cavity. Bake fowl as directed. If there is any remaining mixture, simply bake it in a covered dish that has been sprayed with PAM at 325 degrees for 30 minutes.

This can be used as a side dressing just like Dirty Rice Dressing. However, do not keep any as leftovers and reheat the next day because oysters do not reheat well. Throw any left-overs away.

Notes

Cajun Fish Tail (Tale)

Pascal was telling me how the fish was biting like hell last week at a private lake in North Evangeline. He told me the fish bit so fast and furious that it was necessary for him to go hide behind the pines in order to bait his hook. Some hungry fish jumped in the boat and grabbed the bait right out of his bait bucket, he said. He had to hit them over the head with his oar to keep them out, he said "and in my battle with those crazy, starved creatures, I only caught two small yellow cats, a carp and three perch, me!" he concluded sadly, the grand menteur, him!

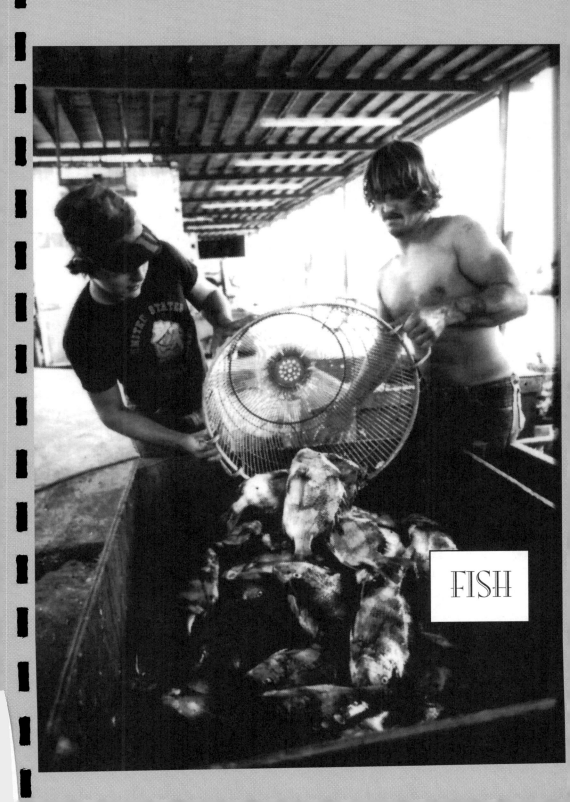

FISH

Catfish Courtbouillon

*My father-in-law
introduced me to this
very simple to prepare
but delicious dish.
This was his specialty.
He always used a big
blue channel catfish
which weighed about
40 pounds because
when he cooked this
he knew he would
have many people
seated at his table
come meal time.*

1	**cup chopped onion**
¾	**cup chopped bell pepper**
¼	**cup chopped celery**
⅔	**cup chopped green onion tops**
	salt and pepper to taste
4-6	**pounds catfish steak**
½	**cup oil**
1	**can tomato soup**

Chop and mix together the onion, bell pepper, celery and onion tops. Season the catfish steaks with salt and pepper to taste. Line the bottom of heavy pot with oil. Layer catfish steaks and chopped mixture until all is used. (Put a catfish layer first then cover with mixed vegetable.) Cover and bring to a slow boil on medium high heat. Uncover and pour the tomato soup on top of last layer. Lower to medium heat. Do not fast boil because the fish will breakup. Allow to cook for 1 hour, partially covered. If gravy is too thin, thicken by mixing ¼ cup water with 1 tablespoon cornstarch, adding hot gravy to cornstarch mixture until well blended, then add to gravy in pot. Serve over rice. Serves 4-6.

This was my father-in-law's recipe. No one could make it as good as he, but I came pretty close.

Fried Catfish

3 cups yellow corn meal
salt & pepper to taste
2-3 pounds catfish filets
oil for frying

Combine cornmeal, salt and pepper. Coat catfish filets well. Drop in deep hot oil, 400 degrees. Fry until golden brown. Serves 4-6

We did not eat much catfish as I was growing up in Gueydan. I guess it was because it was not as plentiful as other seafood or simply because we did not go fishing that often. However, when we did fry catfish we really enjoyed it, and surprisingly enough, we ate it with rice. We used filets but we also fried the whole catfish if they weighed no more than 1½ pounds. The whole catfish is more troublesome to eat, but more tasty.

NOTES

Baked Fish à Mrs. Viyan

I really do not care for baked or broiled fish, but a very dear friend of my mother's taught me how to cook baked fish that anyone would love, even me. Mrs. Viyan Simon actually was my second mom, and she actually contributed to my cooking ability. This is her recipe from way back when. She was also a great fisherman and we always had fresh fish. The first time I went fishing was with her. I caught a huge bowfin (shoo-peek) that almost pulled me into the canal in which we were fishing. Then she took that fish and cleaned it right away and we fried it in a black pot with a fire in a hole which she dug in the ground. That was a real camping experience for me.

4   pounds fresh fish, cleaned, whole
½   cup cooking oil
2   cups chopped onions
1   cup chopped bell pepper
½   cup chopped celery
4   cloves finely chopped garlic
¼   cup sugar
3   tablespoons salt
    salt and black pepper to taste
3   bay leaves
1   10 ounce can Rotel tomatoes
1   8 ounce can stewed tomatoes
2   tablespoons roux
¼   cup white dry wine

Sauté onions, bell pepper, celery and garlic in oil. Add sugar, salt, black pepper, bay leaves, Rotel tomatoes and stewed tomatoes, bring to a boil. Add roux. Lower heat and allow to slow cook for two hours. You may need to add a small amount of water if gravy gets too thick. Pour over fish that has been laid in a large baking dish sprayed with PAM. Add wine. Bake at 375 degrees for 40 minutes. Serves 4-6.

Doc Chandler
Red Fish Filet

2 **pounds Red Fish filets**
salt and pepper to taste
1 **pound lump crab meat**
½ **stick of butter**
¼ **cup cooking wine**
¼ **cup chopped parsley**
1 **tablespoon Worchestershire Sauce**

I recently went to a dermatologist. He was such a nice guy that I will grant his wish to have his recipe in my cookbook. He really is as good a cook as he is a dermatologist.

Season Red Fish with salt and pepper. Lay in a pan covered with foil. Slightly brown under broiler. Remove from oven. Top with crab meat mixture.

Crab Meat Mixture

Sauté crab meat in butter. Add cooking wine, parsley and Worchestershire sauce; mix, pour over fish filets and bake in oven 350 degrees for 10 minutes. Serves 2

Any other types of fish filets may be used to prepare this.

CRABS

You get up at the crack of daylight, equipped with fishing string, salt meat and a dipping net. All along the canals and ditches on the way to Cameron are ideal spots to set up for the day. Make sure you have plenty of food for the day and also drinks such as pop and beer.

On arrival to your choice spot, you quickly tie a small piece of salt meat to the end of a string and throw it into the water. When you feel a tug, you slowly pull up the string, carefully putting the dip net under your catch in the water. Then, you whisk the crabs into a wash tub!

The most exciting part of the day is if you are lucky enough to have two or three crabs "bite" on one line. At the end of the afternoon, your wash tub or ice chest is full and you return on home.

Then, you and your family or friends gather to boil the crabs, a beautiful day having been well fulfilled.

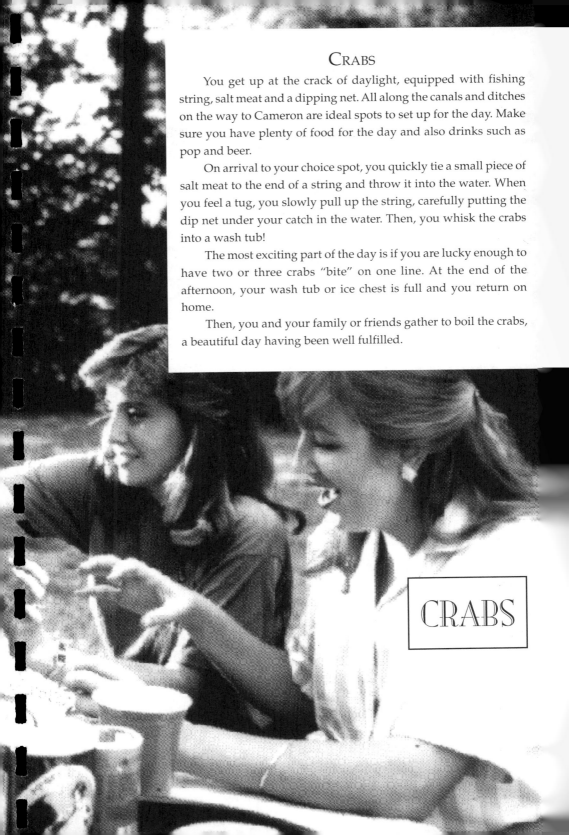

CRABS

Boiled Crabs

Crabs are my favorite seafood. I can never eat enough! In the summer time, my family went crabbing at least once a week. It was a most enjoyable day when all I did was to sit on the bank of a canal or side of a road ditch and pull in gobs of blue crabs. Seems like every bite was as exciting as the last one.

4   **dozen crabs**
    water to cover crabs completely
4   **tablespoon liquid crab boil**
½   **cup salt**
¼   **cup vinegar**

Rinse crabs well with cold water. Add to a pot with enough water to cover crabs completely. Add crab boil, salt and vinegar (the vinegar makes the crabs easier to pick). Bring to a fast boil and boil for 15-20 minutes. Allow to set in water for 5 minutes, then take out of pot.(A mesh insert is good to use and will make it easier to remove crabs.) Spread on a table lined with newspaper or put into large individual platters. Break open the shell and "pick" meat out of crab chambers. This feast is more likely to be enjoyed outside because it is as messy as it is good. Serves 4

NOTES

Crab Meat Au Gratin

⅔ **cup onion, chopped**
¼ **cup bell pepper, chopped**
½ **cup butter or margarine**
3 **tablespoons of flour**
1 **5⅓ ounce can evaporated milk**
   salt & pepper to taste
3 **cups lump crab meat**
¼ **cup parsley, chopped or minced**
½ **cup grated cheese**
2 **tablespoons paprika**

Sauté onion and bell pepper, in margarine or butter. Slowly stir in flour, stirring constantly. Slowly stir in evaporated milk, stirring constantly. Add salt and pepper to taste, crab meat and parsley. Pour into individual foil crab shells or a casserole dish which has been sprayed with PAM. Sprinkle cheese and paprika over the top of casserole. Bake at 350 degrees until hot and bubbly about 20 minutes. Serves 6.

We used to go crabbing along the canals near Cameron. It was a lot of fun and so very good to have a crab boil that evening. When we had some left over, we usually made an au gratin with the meat. I really miss our trips where we made our own nets and baited them with salt pork meat. It was a pleasure that running to the market and buying cleaned crab meat just cannot fulfill.

Stuffed Crabs

One of my sisters-in-law, Bertha Breaux, handed me her own recipe for stuffed crabs. This is the best I have ever eaten.

1 cup onion, chopped
¼ cup bell pepper, finely chopped
5 tablespoons margarine
2 pounds crab meat, preferably fresh
5 slices bread, toasted and dampened
1 egg, beaten
salt & pepper to taste
¼ cup bread crumbs, plain

Sauté onion and bell pepper in margarine until the onion is clear. Add crab meat and sauté together. Take slices of white bread, toasted, and soak in a little water just enough to dampen. Squeeze out the water and break into small pieces. Add the egg to the bread then add the onion and crab meat mixture. Mix thoroughly and season to taste. Put into crab shells (foil ones are available) and bake at 350 degrees for 20 minutes. I usually sprinkle a few bread crumbs on top of each crab before baking. Serves 4

NOTES

Turtle Sauce Piquant

1 cup onion, chopped
1 cup bell pepper, chopped
4 cloves garlic, chopped
¼ cup of oil
1 14 ounce can Rotel tomatoes
1 8 ounce can of tomato sauce
2 tablespoons of tomato paste
¼ cup of roux
2 pounds of turtle meat
  salt and pepper to taste
½ cup green onion tops
¼ cup parsley
2 cups of water

This was my mother's favorite. She would have walked a mile for some turtle meat. I really do not like it much, but I finally did cultivate a taste for the white meat around the turtle's neck—it tastes like chicken or pork.

Sauté onion, bell pepper and garlic in oil. Add Rotel tomatoes, tomato sauce, tomato paste and season to taste with salt and pepper. Cook about thirty minutes, then add roux and water. Add turtle meat, onion tops and parsley and cook for three more hours on a medium heat. Cook until sauce is thick and meat is tender. Add water according to desired thickness of sauce. Serve over rice. Serves 6.

NOTES

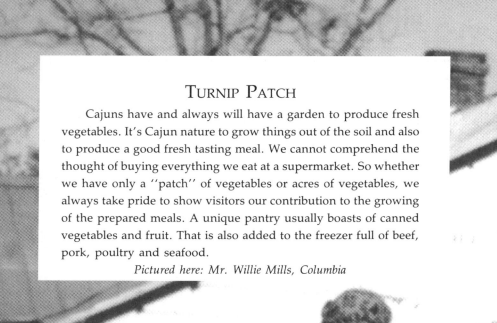

TURNIP PATCH

Cajuns have and always will have a garden to produce fresh vegetables. It's Cajun nature to grow things out of the soil and also to produce a good fresh tasting meal. We cannot comprehend the thought of buying everything we eat at a supermarket. So whether we have only a ''patch'' of vegetables or acres of vegetables, we always take pride to show visitors our contribution to the growing of the prepared meals. A unique pantry usually boasts of canned vegetables and fruit. That is also added to the freezer full of beef, pork, poultry and seafood.

Pictured here: Mr. Willie Mills, Columbia

VEGETABLES

Second Prize Squash Casserole

Another sister-in-law, Janet, entered a rice cookery contest at a fair in Bastrop. She made up this recipe that morning and was delighted when she won second place. This is very quick to prepare and is so tasty. It is definitely one of my favorites.

¾ **cups squash**
¼ **cup water**
1 **pound ground beef**
2 **beaten eggs**
1 **stick margarine**
½ **cup mayonnaise**
1 **cup chopped onion**
1 **cup shredded mild or Velveeta cheese**
1 **cup Ritz cracker crumbs**

Cook squash in water until tender. Drain. Melt butter and add to squash. Cook for 10 minutes, stirring occasionally. Brown beef well with onions in a skillet sprayed with PAM. Season to taste. Mix the two together. Beat eggs and mayonnaise together, and add to beef/squash mixture. Stir well and add cheese. Pour into casserole and cover with cracker crumbs. Bake at 350 degrees until brown, about 15-20 minutes. Serves 4.

If rice is desired, simply add 2 cups of cooked rice before pouring into casserole.

Smothered Turnips

5   cups diced turnips
1   cup water
1   cup chopped onions
1   tablespoon butter
1   tablespoon sugar
    salt and pepper to taste

Wash and peel turnips. Dice. Put the turnips into a saucepan with water and onions. Cook, covered, until the turnips are very tender. Mash down with a potato masher or a large fork. Add butter, salt and pepper to taste. Add sugar. Mix well and cook uncovered on medium heat for 10 minutes. Serves 4.

Cajuns don't cook the greens, only the turnips. My father and I did not like turnips but my mother did. So, naturally, the cook usually cooks what she likes best and my mother was no exception to the rule. So we gradually cultivated a taste for the vegetable. Now, my husband is a great turnip eater and I cook a turnip dish whenever I can get fresh turnips.

Eggplant Casserole à Janet

2   medium eggplants
1   pound smoked sausage, sliced thin
½   cup onions
4   slices dampened bread
1   can cream of mushroom soup
    salt and pepper to taste

Cut eggplant in two. Drop in boiling water and cook until tender. Scoop out pulp. Set aside. Sauté sausage with onions in large skillet which has been sprayed with PAM. Drain well. Add eggplant pulp and mix well. Cook for 4 minutes. Add slices of dampened bread and cream of mushroom soup. Simmer for 5 minutes. Season to taste. Fill eggplant shells. Sprinkle with cracker crumbs and put pats of butter in center. Bake at 350 degrees until hot. Serves 4.

This is a very quick and easy casserole to prepare. My sister-in-law, Janet, shared this with me and I promise it to be a hit at any affair.

Grandmaw's Tomato Sausage

Every Thursday, I would go visit my grandmother. She would always greet me with "On vas avoir un parti!" (We're going to have a party). She would cook sausage in tomato gravy for dinner. Then afterwards, we would walk downtown for a glass of strawberry float. In remembrance of those times, I submit her recipe. This was my favorite.

1 **pound smoked sausage**
¾ **cup oil**
1 **large onion, sliced thin**
1 **large can stewed tomatoes**
   salt and pepper to taste
1 **cup water**

Brown whole links of sausage in oil. Remove from pot. Cut into pieces about an inch long. Remove oil from pot. Add onions and tomatoes. Season to taste. Drop pieces of sausage back into pot with tomato gravy. Cook on medium-high heat for 1 hour, adding a little water at a time. Cook sauce until thick. Serve over rice. Serves 4.

Blackeye Peas

We always served blackeye peas on New Year's Day. If you did, it guaranteed fame and good fortune.

½ **pound dry blackeye peas**
   water to cover peas
¼ **pound sliced bacon or 1 ham bone**
   salt and pepper to taste
½ **cup chopped onions**

Soak dried blackeye peas in water overnight in large saucepan. The next morning, cook peas over medium heat (slow boil) until tender. After about one hour of cooking, add bacon or ham and salt and pepper, and continue to slow boil for at least 30 more minutes or until peas are tender. (You may need to add a dab more of water as you cook.) Just before serving, add finely chopped onions. Serves 4.

Cajun String Beans

1 **16 ounce can cut green beans**
2 **slices bacon, cut in half**
1 **medium potato, diced**
¼ **cup onion, diced**
   salt and pepper to taste
¾ **cup water**

Fry bacon slices until crisp. Add potato. Cook on medium heat for 5 minutes. Add drained can of cut green beans. Season to taste. Add ¾ cup water and cover. Cook on medium low heat for 20 minutes. Serves 4.

Seems that this vegetable was cooked more often than any other. It was a family favorite which everyone enjoyed when I was a girl. It still is!! Now my granddaughter enjoys this vegetable. She has renamed "Chili Beans."

Sweet Potato Casserole

3 **cups mashed sweet potatoes (if using fresh potatoes, bake or boil them before mashing them)**
¾ **cup sugar**
½ **teaspoon salt**
2 **eggs, beaten**
1 **teaspoon vanilla**
3 **tablespoons melted margarine**

Combine all of the above. Spray the casserole with PAM. Pour all ingredients into casserole. Top with mixture below:

½ **cup brown sugar**
⅓ **cup flour**
1 **cup pecans**
1 **cup coconut**
¼ **cup melted margarine**

Mix all above well. Pour over the casserole and bake at 350 degrees for 30 minutes. Serves 6-8.

This is a great dish io bring to a pot luck supper. My sisters-in-law prepare it for camp suppers and I picked up the recipe there. Even canned yams can be used and it is equally as good. This can be used as a dessert, and the children like this also.

Seafood Stuffed Eggplant

I have just recently learned how to prepare this dish. As a cook, I guess I'll never stop learning. This is the way I enjoy serving and eating eggplant the most.

3   eggplants, medium size
⅔   cup water
1   cup chopped onion
½   cup chopped bell pepper
¼   cup butter
1   tablespoon flour
1   pound shrimp, peeled and deveined
8   ounce fresh crab meat
    salt and pepper to taste
¼   cup chopped green onions
4   slices bread soaked in ¼ cup milk
2   cups corn meal
2   eggs, beaten
2   cups flour
    oil for deep frying

Slice eggplants in half. Scoop out pulp, leaving shell ½ inch thick. Set shells aside. Chop pulp and cook in small amount of water until tender. Drain thoroughly. In butter, sauté onions and bell pepper until very limp. Add flour all at once and cook until it is peanut-butter colored. Add salt, pepper and eggplant pulp, cook over medium heat for 20 minutes. Add shrimp and cook for 10 minutes. Add crab meat and green onions and blend. Cook 5 minutes. Add bread that has been soaked in milk and that milk has been squeezed out of to the mixture. Set aside.

In a shallow bowl, add cornmeal. Dredge eggplant shells in flour, shake off excess. Dip into egg that has been beaten. Dredge in cornmeal to coat well. Shake off excess. Gently lower the shell in hot oil and deep fry until golden brown. Drain on paper towel. Stuff with seafood mixture. Serve hot. Serves 6

To shorten preparing time, you may wish to not fry the shell but instead to stuff it with the seafood mixture and bake in oven at 350 degrees for 20 minutes. If you wish to use this method, sprinkle bread crumbs over stuffed shells before baking to prevent drying out.

Broccoli Casserole

½   **cup chopped onion**
½   **cup celery, chopped**
4   **tablespoons butter**
1   **10 ounce package broccoli spears or bits**
1   **10 ounce can cream of mushroom soup**
1   **10 ounce can cream of chicken soup**
1   **cup grated cheese**
2   **cups cooked rice**
    Salt and pepper to taste

Sauté onions and celery in butter. Add broccoli and simmer for 5 minutes. Add cream of mushroom soup, cream of chicken soup, grated cheese and cooked rice. Season. Bake in buttered dish or dish that has been sprayed with PAM at 350 degrees for 30 minutes. Serves 4-6.

My grandmother nor my mother ever baked casseroles. I guess casseroles were not invented when my grandmother cooked and therefore my mother never learned how. That explains why I seldom do prepare casseroles. But this is one that I love to prepare and love to eat. It is so easy to fix.

Cornichon

(pronounced core-nè-shon)

Hot Pickled Cucumbers

10-12   **small hot peppers**
1   **large cucumber**
1   **pint white vinegar**

Wash hot peppers. Slice half of the peppers. Put all the peppers in a quart-size jar.

Peel the cucumber and slice lengthwise into quarters. Add to the jar with the peppers.

Pour vinegar over the cucumber and peppers to fill the jar. Refrigerate for a week before using. Eat with stews, gumbos, sauce piquants, jambalayas, etc., by cutting up the cucumbers into the dish.

Diced peppered cucumbers complement any plate of food.

This is an old time favorite of my family. We always had a jar of Cornichon in our refrigerator, and I still do, especially when my son-in-law, Bernard, or my friends, Lonnie and Freddie enjoy a meal with us. As I use up all the hot pickled cucumbers, I simply add more to the same jar of peppers. These peppers usually last 6-8 months.

Red Beans 'N Rice

This can be prepared with any dried beans and it is always good. Dried beans are much tastier than canned beans, but the secret to their success is to soak them in water the night before. Cajuns never went a week long without cooking a big pot of dried beans.

1 **pound dried red beans**
1 **ham bone or 1 pound smoked sausage that has been sliced**
1 **cup chopped onions**
¼ **cup chopped green onions**
½ **cup chopped green peppers**
   salt and pepper to taste

Wash and sort out beans. Add enough water to cover beans completely in a 4 quart saucepan and soak overnight.

The next morning, heat the beans to a slow boil. Add all the remaining ingredients and cook slowly 3 hours. Add more water during cooking, if necessary. The beans are done when they become soft and the water boils down to form a thick gravy. Season with salt and pepper. Serve over rice. Serves 6.

Corn Maque Choux

15 **ears of clean corn**
1 **cup oil**
2 **cups chopped onion**
1 **cup chopped bell pepper**
2 **large ripe tomatoes, cut up**
1½ **teaspoon salt**
1 **teaspoon sugar**
black pepper to taste

Cut kernels off cob. Heat oil in pot and add corn, onions, bell pepper, tomatoes, salt and sugar. Cook on medium high until it starts to bubble. Lower heat to medium and cook for 1 hour, stirring often to prevent sticking. Pepper to taste. Serves 6.

I can still visualize my father cutting the kernels off of the cob. He did it so patiently and evenly with a sharp knife. Then my mother would roast up a big pot of maque choux. Nothing smells as good nor tastes as good as fresh cooked corn. We always had this on hand as my mother would freeze the corn for us to have throughout the year.

Smothered Okra

1 **pound fresh okra**
1 **cup chopped onion**
½ **cup chopped bell pepper**
1 **large tomato, cut up**
¾ **cup oil**
salt and pepper to taste

Cut up fresh okra. Add all ingredients together in a large skillet and cook until okra is well done, stirring often to prevent sticking. This usually takes about one hour. Serves 6.

We always had fresh okra in our garden. My father sliced it so uniformly. Mama prepared a large pot of smothered okra. She froze the amount which we did not eat at that meal. It kept very well, and was ready to use in any dish whenever we needed it.

Harvest Potato Stew

(Smothered Potatoes)

During the early days of the thrashing crews, that is, when we harvested the rice crop with a thrasher rather than a combine, my mother's favorite meal to fix was a huge pot of potato stew. We fixed a big pot of rice to go with the stew and then brought this to the fields where the crew of men would gather to enjoy. To this day, I still carry the tradition of fixing potato stew for the harvest crew, but not in the same capacity. Potatoes and rice at the same meal were very common at our table.

6   medium potatoes, cut up in small pieces
¼   inch oil in bottom of pot
1   quart of water
    salt and pepper to taste
½   pound cut up sausage or ham
1   cup oil
½   cup chopped onion tops
¼   cup chopped parsley

Heat oil in heavy pot. Add potatoes and brown well. They may stick to the bottom of the pot. If so, simply add a dab of water and continue to brown. While doing this, in another pot, brown the sausage well in oil (if you use ham, just add the ham to the potatoes as they cook). Once the sausage has browned, remove from the pot and cut up into small pieces about ½ inch long. Add to the potatoes and add water. Season to taste. Slow boil for about 30 minutes. Add onion tops and parsley. Cook for another 10 minutes. Serve over rice. Serves 4.

Fried Eggplant

1 **large eggplant, sliced ¼ " thick**
or
2 **large yellow squash, sliced ¼ " thick**
or
10 **medium okras**
2 **beaten eggs**
2 **cups flour**
oil for deep frying, about 2 cups in
a small skillet

This is excellent to accomodate any meat or fish dish. You may also use yellow squash or okra and fry in the same manner. Be sure you serve this hot and always season right after it has been fried.

Wash fresh vegetables and cut up into ¼ inch slices if using eggplant or squash. Okra needs to be sliced in about ½ inch long strips. Dip vegetables into beaten eggs. Roll and coat with flour. Drop into hot oil for frying. Fry until golden brown on all sides. Drain on paper towels. Season with salt and pepper as desired. Serves 3-4.

My Potato Salad

*I never was much of a
potato salad maker.
That is why I am
submitting my recipe
for As-Good-Of-A-
Potato-Salad as I can
make, plus a very
good potato salad
recipe which my
sister-in-law, Agusta
Bollich, makes. That
is her speciality and
we always ask her to
bring it to any of the
family functions or
whenever we have a
covered dish supper.*

3   eggs
4   medium diced potatoes, peeled
¼   cup mayonnaise
2   tablespoons sweet pickle relish
2   tablespoons sugar
    salt and pepper to taste

Boil potatoes and eggs in water until done,
about 20 minutes. Drain. Cool eggs, then peel.
Put potatoes in a salad bowl and add eggs which
you peeled and diced. Add mayonnaise and
sweet relish. Mix thoroughly. Add sugar, salt
and pepper and mix well. I usually serve this at
room temperature but you may wish to refrigerate. Serves 4-6.

Gussie's Best Potato Salad

8   medium potatoes
6   eggs
3   tablespoon sweet pickle relish
2   celery stalks, chopped fine
6   ripe olives, chopped (optional)
    salt and pepper to taste
¾   cups Hellmann's mayonnaise

Boil potatoes with skins in enough water to
cover all. Add eggs and boil for ten minutes or
until potatoes are tender. Allow to cool. Peel
eggs and potatoes and dice. Add relish, celery
and olives. Season to taste. Mix well. Add mayonnaise and mix thoroughly.

Green Salad

1   head lettuce
2   medium tomatoes, sliced
2   medium cucumbers, sliced
1   medium avocado, diced
1   cup sliced mushrooms
1   medium jullienned green pepper
2   stalks chopped celery
1   medium chopped cauliflower

Slice, rinse, and drain lettuce leaves. Add tomatoes, cucumbers, mushrooms, green peppers, celery and cauliflower. Use my special salad dressing to make it perfect.

As I was growing up we seldom had a green salad. And if we did you can bet it came directly from the garden. In later years, I learned to prepare salads from the grocery shelf. This is the one I prepare when I entertain special guests or for special occasions.

Special Salad Dressing

1   cup finely chopped onion
1   cup finely chopped celery
1   cup finely chopped bell pepper
1   cup finely chopped green olives
½   cup olive oil
¼   cup lemon juice
8-10   chopped garlic cloves
2   cans anchovy filets
½   teaspoon oregano
½   teaspoon thyme
½   teaspoon majoram
½   teaspoon savory
3   rosemary leaves
½   teaspoon Worchestershire sauce

Mix all ingredients together in a large tight lidded glass jar. Marinate for 4 days in refrigerator. Several hours before serving, remove from refrigerator and allow to sit at room temperature. Shake well before serving. Spread over green salad. This may be kept indefinitely in the refrigerator, so double the recipe and enjoy.

Ollie's Hot Potato Salad

To me this is the best potato salad anyone can make for any occasion when something different is desired. I learned to make this salad when my sister-in-law, Ollie, shared it with us for one of her delicious meals.

½ **pound bacon, cooked crisp and drippings reserved**
⅓ **cup vinegar and water to make ½ cup**
1 **slightly beaten egg**
1 **teaspoon sugar**
1 **teaspoon salt**
  black pepper to taste
½ **cup chopped green onions**
5 **cups diced cooked potatoes**
1 **tablespoon dijon mustard**

Cook bacon until crisp. Crumble. Combine ⅓ cup bacon drippings with vinegar, egg, sugar, salt, pepper and green onions. Heat slowly and stir until thickened. Add mustard. Pour over potatoes while the potatoes are still hot. Add bacon and stir. Serve immediately. Serves 4.

Cole Slaw

1 **head finely shredded cabbage**
¾ **cup vinegar**
1 **teaspoon salt**
½ **teaspoon pepper**

Shred cabbage finely and refrigerate. Combine vinegar, salt and pepper. Spread over cabbage just before serving. Toss well. Serves 4-6.

We often had cole slaw with our meals but seldom with fried fish. The job of slicing the slaw (cabbage) was always my father's. He had a steady hand and a very sharp knife— both are very important. This is especially good with etouffees or stews.

Sweet Lettuce Salad

16 **small, tender lettuce leaves**
⅓ **cup of vinegar**
½ **cup sugar (enough to cover leaves)**

Wash leaves with cold water and drain. Layer on a platter. Sprinkle vinegar over all the lettuce real well, then sprinkle sugar generously over the leaves. Set platter in refrigerator. Chill until ready to serve. Serves 4.

My parents always had lettuce in the garden. When the leaves were young and tender, Daddy would pick a bunch each day for us to eat. It is sort of awkward to eat (I usually rolled the leaf with my hands to eat it), but it sure tastes good.

SUGAR CANE

Historically, sugar cane growing was a Creole (descendant of French and Spanish colonists) instead of an Acadian (descendants of those exiled from the 18th Century Acadia) vocation. Today, however, Cajuns grow much of the cane in Louisiana's sugar belt. Sugar cane fields stretch out as far west as several miles out of Kaplan.

It is a hard crop to raise. The first year, plants must be planted by hand. The same plant is used for three crops. These are called "stubbles" and reproduce after being harvested three times. (One planting makes three crops.) Just before harvest, the priests bless the crops at an annual ceremony. Then as the crop is harvested, the cut cane must be loaded onto a wagon to be taken to a sugar mill such as is pictured. Of course, now modern trucks are used to haul the sugar cane.

The tall, beautiful sugar cane stalk is the most beautiful product in south Louisiana. Thousands of acres stream out across the bayou land plantations.

DESSERTS

Tête Rouge Cake

While in college, my son asked me to bake a cake from a recipe which he had gotten from one of his lady friends. He claims he could not remember her name, but since she had red hair, we have since called it Tete Rouge Cake, red head cake. Actually, it is an Orange Mandarin Cake.

1 box Pillsbury yellow cake mix with pudding mix inside
1 teaspoon baking powder
1 cup oil
4 beaten eggs
1 teaspoon vanilla
1 10 ounce can mandarin orange sections, juice included
  oil and flour for coating
  string of sewing thread

Pour cake mix in a large bowl. Add baking powder, oil and eggs. Beat well together on medium high for two minutes, scraping sides occasionally. Add vanilla flavoring and beat one more minute. Add can of mandarin orange sections plus juice and mix by hand until well blended. Pour into two 9 inch round cake pans which have been well floured and greased, or sprayed with PAM if you prefer, and bake at 350 degrees for 45 minutes. Remove from pans and cool on wire racks or large dinner plates. Take a long string of sewing thread and slice each layer with it, going across the layers towards you in a slow sawing motion. Lay out on a cake plate and spread each layer with frosting below.

Frosting
1 20 ounce can crushed pineapple
1 3¼ ounce package vanilla pudding (instant)
1 9 ounce cool whip

Mix well crushed pineapple with juice, instant vanilla pudding and cool whip. Stir until well blended. Spread over each layer. Refrigerate.

Lucy's Baptismal Cake

½ cup butter
¼ cup whipping cream
1 cup brown sugar
¼ cup coarsely chopped pecans
1 box Pillsbury Chocolate cake mix
1¼ cup water
⅓ cup oil
3 eggs
1¾ cup whipping cream
¼ cup powdered sugar
1 teaspoon vanilla
   pecans to garnish
   chocolate curls to garnish

For Cajuns, to baptize an infant or an adult calls for a big celebration. To celebrate is what Cajuns love to do the most. So after my newborn granddaughter's baptismal ceremony at the church, we gathered at my home to do just that, celebrate. A lot of in-laws and friends on both sides of my granddaughter's family were present. We enjoyed a lot of conversation, wine and dining. Grandmother Sue McKenzie had brought the most delicious cake I had ever tasted. She called it a caramel cake, but I have renamed it a Baptismal Cake.

Heat oven to 325 degrees. In a small heavy saucepan, combine butter or margarine, whipping cream and brown sugar. Cook over low heat until butter is melted, stirring occasionally. Pour into two 9 or 8 inch round cake pans. Sprinkle evenly with chopped pecans. In a large bowl, combine chocolate cake mix, water, oil and eggs at a low speed until moistened. Beat 2 minutes on high. Carefully spoon batter over pecan mixture. Bake at 325 degrees for 35 to 45 minutes or until cake springs back when touched in center or when a toothpick comes out clean when stuck in center of layers. Cool 5 minutes. Remove from pans and cool completely. In a small bowl, beat whipping cream until it forms soft peaks. add powdered sugar and vanilla. To assemble cake, place one layer on cake plate, praline side up. Spread with half whipped cream mixture. Place second layer on top of first and cover with remainder of whipped cream mixture. Garnish with pecans and chocolate curls. Refrigerate.

Red Velvet Cake

My daughters always preferred this cake to any other I made. Of course, baking cakes is not one of my specialties. This is the one they always asked me to bring to friends. I usually had to bake their cakes. When my oldest daughter got married, she wanted her wedding cake to be a red velvet cake. However, being that the wedding was not around Christmas, I suggested she get another kind.

½ cup butter
1½ cups sugar
3 eggs
3 tablespoons cocoa (Hershey's)
2 ounces red food coloring
2½ cups flour
1 teaspoon salt
1 cup buttermilk
1 teaspoon vanilla
2 ounces water
1 teaspoon baking soda
1 teaspoon vinegar

Cream butter and sugar until fluffy. Add eggs, beating well. Mix a paste of cocoa and food coloring. Add to batter alternately with buttermilk, vanilla and water. Add soda. Blend well and then stir in vinegar. Do not beat. Pour into 2 nine inch greased and floured round cake pans. Bake at 350 degrees for 45 minutes. Frost with fluffy butter frosting or cream cheese frosting (see page 108).

Quick and Easy But Delicious Red Velvet Cake

1 **box Duncan Hines Yellow Cake Mix (No pudding in the mix)**
½ **cup sugar**
2 **tablespoons cocoa**
½ **cup oil**
4 **eggs**
1 **ounce red food coloring**
1 **cup milk plus 1 tablespoon vinegar**

Mix all above. Bake in two 9 inch pans at 350 degrees for thirty minutes. Cool on wire rack. (Cut into four layers or leave as two large layers.) Frost with fluffy butter frosting or cream cheese frosting (see page 108).

This recipe is a blessing for red velvet cake lovers. One of my nieces made this cake for a family get-together, so now, when I bake a cake, it is usually this one. It makes great Christmas gifts when you want to give a special gift to someone and help out with the hum-drum of baking at the same time.

NOTES

_____

_____

_____

_____

_____

_____

_____

Fluffy Butter Frosting

- 6 tablespoon flour
- 1½ cup milk
- ¾ cup butter
- 1½ cup sugar
- 1 teaspoon vanilla flavoring

Mix flour and milk and cook until thick, stirring constantly with wire whisk. Cool. Cream butter, sugar and vanilla until fluffy. Add milk mixture and blend well. Spread on cake layers.

Cream Cheese Frosting

- 1 16 ounce package powdered sugar
- 1 8 ounce package softened Philadelphia Cream Cheese
- ½ cup softened butter
- 1 teaspoon vanilla flavoring (Watkins)
- 1 cup chopped nuts

Cream the first four ingredients until well blended. Stir in pecans. Spread on cake.

NOTES

Lucy's Coconut Cake

1 box white Duncan Hines cake mix
¼ cup cooking oil
1 8 ounce carton sour cream
3 eggs, beaten
1 8 ounce can Lopez Cream of
   Coconut

Mix all of the above ingredients. Pour into greased and floured 9"x13" pan. Bake at 350 degrees for 30 minutes. Cool. Top with icing.

Icing

1 box powdered sugar (1 pound)
¼ cup butter
2 tablespoons milk
2 teaspoons vanilla flavoring
1 8 ounce cream cheese, softened
1 cup shredded coconut

Mix all ingredients, except coconut, well; spread on cake. Top with coconut.

Bertha's Jelly Rolls

4 eggs
1 teaspoon vanilla
¾ cup sugar
¾ cup flour
¼ teaspoon salt
¾ teaspoon baking powder
1 cup powdered sugar
½ pint jelly of your preference

Beat eggs. Add sugar and vanilla. Cream well. Add flour, salt and baking powder. Blend well. Pour onto waxed paper-lined jelly roll pan. Bake at 375 degrees for 13 minutes. Take out and roll in towel dusted with powdered sugar. Let stand for 5 minutes. Unroll and spread jelly on top, then re-roll. Refrigerate until served.

I am not much of a cake baker, but I do force myself to serve a coconut cake at family gatherings or when friends come to enjoy a meal with us. This recipe is especially for my friend, Carolyn Vereen, who recently reminded me of the many times I would bake this cake when we were together. It is delicious and very easy to make; even a special member of the Gourmet Club has successfully baked it!

My husband's oldest sister cannot be beat when it comes to cooking. She started cooking when she was high enough to reach the stove. She excelled in many dishes but her jelly rolls were and still are a favorite among us.

Almond Cheesecake

For Christmas, 1993, I decided to invest in a spring form pan by Revere.I had never used one before so it was something new for me. So I also used a new recipe which I found inside the pan. Needless to say, this was a big success. My sister-in-law, Janet, actually accused me of ordering it from New York. That was a big compliment to me.

Crust
4   ounces butter or margarine
1   cup sugar
2   eggs
2   cups flour
1   teaspoon baking powder

Add ingredients in order, blending together to make a soft dough. Press into Revere spring form pan (10"/26 centimeter pan) Set aside.

Filling
2   eggs
12 ounces cream cheese at room temperature
¾   cup sugar
1   teaspoon lemon juice
1   teaspoon almond extract

Beat eggs. Blend in cream cheese. Mix sugar,lemon juice and almond extract,adding to cheese mixture. Beat until creamy. Pour into prepared crust and bake 30 minutes at 350 degrees. Cool 5 minutes.

Sour Cream Topping
3   tablespoon sugar
1   teaspoon lemon juice
1   teaspoon almond extract
1   cup sour cream

Mix ingredients and spread on baked cheesecake. Bake 10 minutes at 350 degrees. Sprinkle with slivered almonds.

Pecan Pie

4   beaten eggs
⅔ cup sugar
1   cup light Karo syrup
1   cup pecan halves or pieces
1   teaspoon vanilla flavoring, Watkins

Beat eggs slightly. Add sugar and beat until dissolved. Stir in Karo syrup and vanilla flavoring. Add pecans. Mix well and pour into unbaked 9 inch pie shell and bake at 400 degrees for 15 minutes. Reduce heat to 325 degrees and bake for 45 minutes or until a knife inserted in center comes out clean. Cool before serving or serve warm with a large scoop of vanilla ice cream. Serves 6.

My husband's brother, Raymond, brought this recipe home from the seminary. I really serve this pie more often than any other dessert. It is so quick and easy to make. It is also everyone's favorite. Fresh pecans are always best to use.

Pie Shell

1¼ cup flour
½   teaspoon salt
⅓   cup Crisco
3-4 teaspoon cold water

Mix flour and salt. Cut in Crisco with pastry blender or knives. Add water until all dough is moistened. Form into a ball. On a lightly floured board, flatten dough with hands. Roll out dough from center to edge, forming a circle about 12 inches in diameter. Place in 9 inch pie plate. Prick bottom and side with a fork. Bake in 425 degrees oven for 10-12 minutes or until golden brown. Cool.

Lemon Meringue Pie

This is my best lemon pie recipe. It cannot be beat and it is simple to make. I always use fresh lemon juice. This was also my mother's favorite pie, even though she seldom baked. She always left the baking to me.

1½ cup sugar
7 tablespoons cornstarch
⅛ teaspoon salt
1½ cup water
3 egg yolks, beaten
2 tablespoons butter or margarine
½ cup lemon juice
9 inch cooked pastry shell
3 egg whites
1 teaspoon lemon juice
6 tablespoon sugar

Combine sugar, cornstarch and salt in saucepan. Stir in water. Stir until dissolved and bring to a boil over medium heat. Cook, stirring constantly until it thickens, about 5 minutes. Remove from heat. Stir in small amount of hot mixture into beaten egg yolks, then pour back into saucepan. Bring to a boil and cook for 1 minute, stirring constantly. Remove from heat. Add butter and slowly add lemon juice. Stir to blend evenly. Cool to lukewarm and pour into cooled pastry shell. Beat egg whites until they form soft peaks. Gradually add sugar and lemon juice, beating well. Spread over cooled pie. Bake in 400 degree oven for 10 minutes. Cool thoroughly and refrigerate until ready to serve. Serves 6.

Blueberry Pie

8 ounce Philadelphia Cream Cheese
1 cup granulated sugar
8 ounce cool whip
1 pint raw fresh blueberries

Cream together the cream cheese and sugar. Add cool whip and mix well. Add blueberries and fold into cream cheese mixture. Pour into baked pie shell and refrigerate over night. Strawberries or peaches may be used as a substitute for the fruit.

Pie Crust
1⅓ cup plain flour
½ teaspoon salt
½ cup Crisco Shortening
3 tablespoon cold water
½ cup pecan pieces

Sift flour and salt. Add Crisco and cut in with a pastry cutter or two knives for pea-size consistency. Add water. Work in together. Roll out on lightly floured pastry board and put in a 9 inch pie pan. Bake at 350 degrees for about 10 minutes then sprinkle pecan pieces over the bottom of crust and continue to bake until the crust turns golden brown. Cool completely before adding filling.

This is the dessert that a very dear friend, Vickie Gregory, prepared when I entertained a delegation of Japanese representing a restaurant firm in Japan. They were interested in Cajun cooking, so I introduced them to just that. The rest of the menu consisted of fish courtboullion, green salad with my special dressing, crawfish bisque, shrimp casserole, string beans, mixed fruit salad, crawfish mold served as an appetizer and this delicious pie for dessert. They thoroughly enjoyed the tour of our rice fields and, of course, the meal.

Coconut Pie

This is my specialty dessert. I always make this when family comes or for special occasions. It is also my husband's and my son's favorite. I used to always have a coconut pie baked when my husband would come to court me. I was taught that the way to a man's heart was through his stomach. It works.

²/₃ **cup flour**
¾ **cup sugar**
2 **cups milk**
4 **medium separated eggs**
1½ **teaspoons Watkins vanilla flavoring**
1½ **cups Baker's coconut flakes**

Mix flour and sugar in a deep sauce pan. Add milk and heat until it comes to a slow boil, stirring constantly. When it starts to thicken, add the beaten egg yolks to ¼ cup hot mixture. Mix well and return to mixture in saucepan. Cook on medium heat stirring constantly until it thickens. This takes about 5 minutes. Remove from heat and add vanilla flavoring. Stir well, add coconut and mix well. Pour into baked pie shell. Top with egg white meringue and bake at 400 degrees for 10 minutes. Serves 6

Easy Coconut Pie

This recipe was given to me by my sister-in-law, Barbara Ann. She has never been fond of cooking (seems like all the Barbaras in the family feel the same way). However, when they do, their dishes are very tasty.

3 **well-beaten eggs**
1¼ **cup sugar**
½ **cup milk**
2 **tablespoons melted butter**
¼ **teaspoon salt**
1 **teaspoon vanilla**
2 **cups coconut flakes**
1 **9-inch pie shell**

Beat eggs and sugar until well blended. Mix in all other ingredients. Pour into uncooked pie shell. Bake at 350 degrees for 1 hour or until done. Serves 6.

Chocolate Pie

1   cup sugar
⅓   cup flour
3   tablespoons cocoa (Hersheys)
⅛   teaspoon salt
3   egg yolks
2   cups milk
¼   cup butter
1   teaspoon Vanilla

Mix all dry ingredients, mixing sugar and cocoa first. Slowly add milk. Bring to a slow boil. Add beaten egg yolks and melted butter. Bring to a boil until it thickens, stirring constantly. Remove from heat. Add vanilla flavoring (Watkins) and beat well. Cool. Pour into a cooked 9 inch pie crust. Top with meringue or cool whip.

My son-in-law's favorite pie is chocolate (anything with chocolate is his favorite) and it is also my brother's favorite. So I have had a lot of practice baking this pie. I sort of like it myself.

Meringue For Pies

3 or 4   egg whites, stiffly beaten
½   cup sugar

Beat egg whites until they are stiff and form high peaks. Slowly add sugar. Beat at medium speed for about 1 minute. Immediately spread meringue over pie, carefully sealing to edge of pastry to prevent shrinkage. Bake at 400 degrees for 10 minutes or until browned.

Pineapple Dumplings

1½ **cups flour**
½ **cup Crisco**
½ **cup water**
½ **cup sugar**
1 **15¼ ounce can crushed pineapple,
   drain juice and save**
½ **cup water**
⅓ **cup sugar**
¼ **cup margarine, cut into small pieces**

Cut the Crisco into the flour. Add water to form
a sticky dough. Roll out on slightly floured
board. Sprinkle sugar on top and spread the
drained crushed pineapple over entire dough
that is about ¼ inch thick. Roll and refrigerate.
In bottom of baking dish, add the pineapple
juice, water and sugar. Take dough and slice
into ½ inch thickness. Place in juice, dot with
butter and bake at 325 degrees for 30 minutes.
Serves 6.

Watermelon Rind Preserves

1 small watermelon
6 cups sugar

Slice watermelon after you have eaten the red inside. Peel the rind off the slices and cut the slices in chunks. Put them in a large pot and add sugar on top of chunks. Allow to slow boil for several hours (about 4 hours) stirring occasionally. When chunks are tender and juice is thick enough, spoon the preserves in scalded jars. Pour juice in to fill jars. Seal tightly and store. Yields about 4 pints.

As you have read, Cajuns did not throw anything away, not even the watermelon rinds. This is my favorite way to cook them. I always enjoyed a bowl of couch-couch with watermelon rind preserves.

Maw Maw Z's Blackberry Jelly

1 gallon blackberry juice
sugar to equal the amount of juice used
or
1 cup blackberry juice
1 cup sugar

Put one cup of juice in a boiler. Stir in 1 cup sugar and allow to boil slowly, stirring occasionally. As soon as the juice forms a thick syrup when dropped from the spoon into a cup of cold water, the jelly is done (about 20 minutes). Pour immediately into pint jars that have been scalded. Seal tightly and store on pantry shelf. Always fill each jar to the top.

If you have fresh blackberries, use a juicer to squeeze the juice out, and be sure to throw away the seeds.

My mother-in-law is the world's greatest blackberry picker and jelly maker. We often had homemade bread and homemade blackberry jelly. It's from her that I learned to make this jelly. She never doubled the recipe.

Nan Nan's Fig Tarts

This is an old family recipe. My Godmother, Mrs. Eve Gaspard, made the best tarts I have ever tasted. This is her recipe. I have not yet been able to make mine taste as good as hers. Maybe, someday, when I get to be her age, or have as much practice as she had. I can succeed as well as she. Her four daughters are all great tart makers also.

1   pint fig preserves or fresh figs which have been mashed down.
½   teaspoon nutmeg, ground fresh. Mix nutmeg with mashed fresh figs and refrigerate overnight.
2   cups sugar
⅛   teaspoon salt
½   teaspoon nutmeg, fresh ground
1½   teaspoon baking powder
2½   sticks butter, softened to room temperature
1   tablespoon Crisco
6   medium eggs or 5 large eggs
1   teaspoon Vanilla flavor, Watkins
⅔   cup Carnation evaporated milk, pure
3-4   cups flour

In a large bowl mix well the sugar, salt, nutmeg and baking powder. Add butter and Crisco and beat well. Add eggs, one at a time and beat well till the mixture is creamed very fine. Add vanilla flavor and Carnation milk and mix well. Add the flour slowly till the dough reaches the right consistency to be able to roll out. The dough must not be too stiff (I usually leave it a little soft). On a well floured board, put a large tablespoon (heaping) of dough. Knead by hand until you can press it down with your hand. Roll it out till it reaches the size you want it to be (about the size of a small saucer). Put figs or preserves on half of the rolled dough. Bring over the other half of the tart and press down the sides shut carefully. Do each of the tarts in that manner. Using a spatula, pick up each of the tarts carefully and lay on a large cookie sheet which has been covered with foil or sprayed with PAM. Make sure tarts are not too close to
Continued on next page

each other — about one inch apart. Bake at 375 degrees for about 15 minutes or until tarts reach a dark golden brown color. Remove immediately from baking sheet and cool. Makes about one dozen. These may be frozen in a Zip-Loc bag.

Vanilla Homemade Ice Cream

8 **beaten eggs**
3 **cups sugar**
3 **12 ounce cans Pet milk**
1 **tablespoon vanilla flavoring (I recommend Watkins)**
  milk to equal 3 Pet cans full
  ice cubes
  salt to cover ice in the bucket

Beat eggs well. Add sugar and cream well. Add Pet milk and pour in a large, deep pot. Add milk and cook over medium heat about 20 minutes—do not scald. Remove from heat and add vanilla flavoring. Cool. Pour into inner ice cream bucket. Place in outer freezer bucket. Add ice until bucket is full, pouring salt over each layer of ice. Begin to turn until motor shuts off or until bucket feels very heavy to turn. Allow to set for 25 minutes. Serve immediately or freeze.

Fruit can be added to cooked mixture after it cools.

This was always a treat as I was growing up. My mother would cook the ingredients and I would help my father freeze the ice cream. He would always put a heavy towel over the freezer just to keep the chill off so I could sit on top while he turned the handle of the freezer. There were no electric ones then. Why I sat on the freezer, I will never know. I guess it was to keep me from getting into trouble with the ice and salt. Nonetheless, I always enjoyed helping and even more so eating it. Once it was done, my mother always had the inner paddle to scrape the ice cream off of. That was all she ever ate.

Old Style Rice Pudding

*Another regular at
our house was rice
pudding. This is
always a hit
regardless who is
being served.*

3 **well beaten eggs**
⅔ **cups sugar**
¼ **teaspoon salt**
3 **cups scalded milk**
⅓ **cup butter**
2 **cups cooked rice, cooled**
¾ **cup raisins or 1 cup cooked apples**
1 **teaspoon vanilla, Watkins**
⅛ **teaspoon cinnamon**
⅛ **teaspoon nutmeg**

Combine eggs, sugar and salt and cream well.
Gradually add scalded milk. Add butter, rice
raisins, vanilla, cinnamon and nutmeg. Mix
thoroughly. Pour into 1 quart casserole sprayed
with PAM. Set in shallow pan which has about
1 inch water in it or set a pan of water beneath
the casserole while it is baking. This prevents
pudding from drying out while baking. Bake
at 325 degrees for 1½ hours. Serves 4-6.

Notes

Old Style Bread Pudding

8 **slices bread, 3-4 days old or French Bread is even better**
3 **cups milk**
2 **tablespoon butter**
3 **beaten eggs**
½ **cup sugar**
½ **teaspoon salt**
¼ **cup raisins (optional)**
¾ **cups cooked apples (optional)**

Scald milk and butter together on stove or in microwave on high for 2 minutes. Beat eggs, salt and sugar together. Add scalded milk mixture. Add raisins or apples if desired. Break bread into small pieces and put into buttered 13 inch by 9 inch pan. Pour mixture over bread and bake in 325 degree oven for 45 minutes. Place a pan of water beneath the baking dish while in the oven. This keeps your pudding moist.

I prefer to use French Bread instead of plain bread, so when I do, I soak it in the milk the night before I bake my pudding.

We never threw anything away at home. So as the bread got older, or less fresh, we would use it in bread puddings. My father was not a sweet eater, but bread pudding, rice pudding and gingerbread he did like.

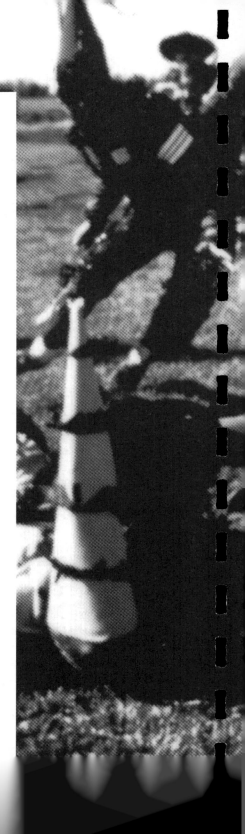

Mardi Gras

Mardi Gras is celebrated the day before the religous feast of Ash Wednesday, which marks the first day of Lent.

In the southwest Louisiana countryside, bands of masked and costumed horsemen visit area farms to request a chicken for a big gumbo to be served just before the dance in town that night.

The Mardi Gras, as they are called, must run the chicken down to justify the catch. If not enough chickens are caught, then they must beg for money to go purchase chickens for their big gumbo. Everyone returns to a designated spot, cleans the chickens and prepares their feast. Everyone enjoys the beer, gumbo, boasting and dancing until midnight.

In New Orleans, however, Mardi Gras is feted at a different pace.

The carnival season begins on January 6 and vibrates forward within the liturgical cycle up to Shrove Tuesday just prior to the solemn penitential days of Lent.

People enjoy grabbing for the throws of the old-line krewes of Carnival such as Comus, Rex and Proteus. These krewes form the core of the Anglo-Creole aristocratic social structure of the city. In the streets, they parade as royalty and at their private balls, they project the royal image with strict guest lists, formal rules, debutantes and tableaux.

On the streets, Mardi Gras is another story. Anyone has the opportunity to costume elaborately and get a chance to throw beads from truck floats. Different classes of people and many cultures emerge from the crowded parade streets. Everyone has a wild time!

MARDI GRAS

King's Cake

No Creole or Cajun cookbook is complete without a recipe for a king's cake. They are very popular all over the entire state of Louisiana. It originated in South Louisiana, mainly in New Orleans, and made its way up to Monroe, Louisiana. There are several variations of stories that depict the purpose of the contents of the cake— if a baby doll is used, and you find it, you will be the next one to have a party. If a dime is used, you will be the next millionaire. If a fertility bean is used, you will have the next baby. Regardless of what you find in a king's cake, you will enjoy eating it. They are most popular at Mardi Gras, reflecting the King of Mardi Gras.

Brioche Dough

1   cup scalded milk
1   cup butter
2/3 cup sugar
1   teaspoon salt
1/4 cup warm water
1   package yeast
2   beaten egg yolks
6   beaten whole eggs
6   cups sifted flour

Scald milk. Cool to lukewarm. Cream butter. Add sugar and salt and cream together. Sprinkle yeast over water in a large bowl. Stir until dissolved. Stir in milk and creamed mixture. Add beaten egg yolks, whole beaten eggs and sifted flour. Beat 10 minutes. Cover. Let rise for about 2 hours or until double in bulk. Stir down and beat well with fists. Turn over as you beat. Cover tightly and refrigerate overnight. Stir down and turn out soft dough on slightly floured board. Knead and form into a roll about 12 inches long. Place on a baking sheet that has been sprayed with PAM. Form into a ring. Press down the dime, doll or bean so it is completely covered. Let rise again for about an hour. When ready to bake, brush with mixture of egg whites and sugar. Bake in 375 degrees oven for 25-35 minutes or until golden brown. Cool on wire rack.

Sugars
green, purple and yellow food
coloring pastes
12 **tablespoons granulated sugar**

Prepare the colored sugars by squeezing a dab of paste in the palm of one hand. Sprinkle 2

Continued on next page

tablespoons of sugar over the paste and rub your hands together to color the sugar evenly. Set aside and repeat the process with green, then twice with purple and yellow (do not mix sugars). Using the already prepared colored sugars is much easier, however may not be attainable in certain areas.

Icing
3 cups confectioners sugar
1/4 cup fresh lemon juice
3-6 tablespoon water
2 candied cherries

When the cake has cooled, prepare the icing. Combine the confectioners sugar, lemon juice and 3 tablespoons water in a deep bowl. Stir until smooth. Add 1 teaspoon water until desired consistency is reached and can be easily spread on the ring. Spread icing over the top with a spatula, allowing it to run over the sides of the cake. Sprinkle the colored sugars over the icing immediately, forming a row of purple, a row of yellow and a row of green stripes about 1 inch apart on both sides of the ring. Garnish with cherries at each end of the cake.

BREADS

Bought bread was not common at home.

Mama always mixed her bread dough before she went to bed. Then, it would rise overnight. The next morning, the dough would be overlapping the sides of the bowl. It was my job and pleasure to "beat" the dough down so Mama could get it into the bread pans.

I still use the same bowl and pans which she baked her bread in. The smell of freshly baked bread is heavenly.

BREADS

Chef's Homemade Bread

This is one of the foods that my mother-in-law taught me to make which was better than my mother's. There were twelve children in the Zaunbrecher family, but my mother-in-law did not like to cook. Luckily, she always had a daughter who did. Chef Hans always brags about my rolls, and that is a big compliment. Every time he visits, I have some baked.

1	cup milk
3	tablespoons sugar
2½	teaspoons salt
6	tablespoons oil
1	cup warm water
1	package Fleischmann's Yeast
6	cups sifted all-purpose flour

Scald milk. Pour into a large bowl. Stir in sugar, salt, and oil. Cool to lukewarm. Measure warm water in another small bowl. Sprinkle in yeast and stir until dissolved. Stir into lukewarm milk mixture. Add 3 cups all-purpose flour. Beat until smooth. Stir in additional 3 cups of flour. Knead inside of bowl, having added about 3 tablespoons oil in bottom of bowl with dough. Knead until smooth and elastic. Cover with damp cloth. Let rise until double in size. Punch down and allow to rise again until double in size. Repeat. Having punched it down for the fourth time, shape into large rolls about the size of a lemon, or divide into two loaves. Place in well oiled baking pans and allow to rise until double in size. Bake in hot oven 400 degrees about 35 minutes.

This procedure takes almost all day so I usually start around 9:00 A.M.and the bread is ready to bake around 6:00 P.M. It is well worth the time and effort. Nothing is as good as fresh homemade bread, butter and homemade blackberry jelly.

Mrs. Broussard's French Pancakes

1 **cup milk**
2 **tablespoons butter or oil**
2 **eggs, beaten**
½ **cup sifted flour**
1 **teaspoon baking powder**
½ **teaspoon salt**

Heat together the milk and butter. Allow to cool. Beat eggs and add to cooled milk and butter. Mix flour, baking powder and salt. Add flour to mixture. Whip until smooth. Pour into desired thickness and size of pancake or crepe in a heated skillet that has been sprayed with PAM or lined with oil. Flip over and cook on the other side after the batter is firm enough to turn, usually you can tell when it is ready by the edges turning up or appearing dry. Serves 2.

A friend from Cameron Parish came to visit one night and introduced me to this delicious pancake recipe. His mother, Mrs. Clara Ellender Broussard, had given him this recipe which she would fix for her family. We prepared it that night for my family and a group of friends. I was not used to eating pancakes for supper, but as it turned out, I have done so several times since. This recipe can be used for pancakes or for crepes, spreading the batter out thinner for crepes.

Notes

Eggs Bread à la Linda

2   tablespoons butter
1   slice bread
1   whole egg
     salt and pepper to taste

Melt butter in a small skillet. Take a piece out of the center of the bread. Drop the piece in the skillet and lay the slice of bread in the center of the skillet. Break open the egg and drop it in the center of the bread where the hole is. Allow to cook on medium heat until bread toasts on one side. Carefully flip over on the other side and slightly toast on that side. Remove from skillet and serve hot. Season to taste. This is for a soft egg yolk. If you like a hard yolk, simply break the yolk as soon as you drop the egg in the center of the bread. Serves one.

Cornbread

1¼   cups cornmeal
  3   teaspoons baking powder
  1   tablespoon sugar
  1   large egg, beaten
  1   cup milk
  3   tablespoons oil

Sift dry ingredients together. Make a well in center. Beat egg, milk, and oil together and pour into the well. Mix thoroughly. Pour into heated, well-greased round 8 inch skillet and bake at 400 degrees for 20-25 minutes or until mixture pulls away from the pan.

Creole Rice Calas

½ cup warm water
3 tablespoons sugar
1 ¼ ounce package active dry yeast
2 cups cooked white rice
3 eggs, slightly beaten
1½ cups sifted all-purpose flour
½ teaspoon salt
1 teaspoon vanilla (Watkins)
¼ teaspoon nutmeg, fresh vegetable oil for frying
2 cups sugar
2 tablespoons cinnamon

Even though this is not of Cajun origin, I really like these rice doughnuts. My friend, Chef Hans, introduced me to these and I cannot fix them often enough. They are real good and also gives another way to prepare rice. This is good to serve at a New Orleans-style brunch to add a note of authenticity. It is also a great way to use left-over rice.

The night before you serve the calas, combine water and sugar in a glass bowl. Stir in yeast. Let stand until foamy, 5-10 minutes. In a medium bowl, combine yeast mixture and rice. Cover bowl with plastic wrap, set aside in a warm place overnight. This step forms a starter for calas. In the morning, stir rice mixture thoroughly. Add eggs, flour, salt, vanilla and nutmeg. Beat with a wooden spoon until combined. Cover with plastic and let rise in a warm place. Heat oil in a large saucepan over medium high. Drop rice mixture by rounded tablespoons into hot oil. Fry until golden brown (5-6 minutes) on both sides. Drain calas on paper towels. Shake in a paper bag with 2 cups sugar and 2 tablespoons of cinnamon. Serve hot. Makes 24.

You may substitute powdered sugar for cinnamon/ sugar mix.

Gingerbread

(Lu Mas Pain)

This was one of my favorites as a young girl. I enjoyed this in the morning as a quick bite before leaving for school or as a snack after school. A tall glass of cold milk always accompanied a piece of Mama's gingerbread.

1   cup brown sugar
1   tablespoon baking soda
1   teaspoon salt
1   teaspoon allspice
1   teaspoon cinnamon
1   teaspoon ground cloves
1   teaspoon ginger
3   eggs
1   cup dark cane syrup
1   cup soft margarine
2¾ cups all purpose flour
1   cup hot water

Combine all dry ingredients in a large mixing bowl. Mix in eggs, cane syrup, and margarine. Beat well. Add flour slowly beating well. Add hot water. Beat until smooth. Pour into 2-9 inch lightly greased and floured round cake pans, or 1 sheath cake pan that has been lightly greased and floured. Bake at 350 degrees for 45 minutes. Serve warm or cold. Will keep for several days in tightly closed container.

NOTES

Doughnuts

(Croquinoles - Kro-Ce-Yoils)

½ **cup butter**
1¾ **cup sugar**
1 **teaspoon vanilla (Watkins)**
3 **eggs**
1 **cup milk**
4 **teaspoon baking powder**
⅛ **teaspoon salt**
4 **cups flour**
   oil for deep frying
   confectioners sugar for coating

Beat butter and sugar until light and fluffy. Add flavoring. Add one egg at a time, beating well after each. Add milk and mix well. Mix all dry ingredients and add to the egg mixture slowly, beating well. Place dough on a well floured board. Roll to ¾ inch thick. Cut into rounds with a very small glass or small cutter. Fry in hot oil 400 degrees until lightly brown on both sides. Put sugar into a large paper bag. Drop fried doughnuts into the bag and shake to coat. Serve warm. Makes about 3 dozen.

It was always a treat at Mardi Gras for us to go to my in-laws for doughnuts. My mother-in-law made doughnuts for the whole family, 11 children their mates and children. Late that afternoon, we all came in and enjoyed this wonderful treat. She did not cut the doughnuts, but instead just fried a whole round ball of dough about the size of a small egg. Regretfully, I have not kept up the tradition.

NOTES

French Toast

(Pain Perdue)

This was and is still great for breakfast. My father always prepared this for us. He would fry the bread in a skillet lined with grease, but now I grill the soaked bread instead. No matter how it is fixed, it's good.

2   eggs well beaten
⅔   cup sugar
½   teaspoon Watkins vanilla flavoring
3   slices of bread
½   cup oil
    powdered sugar to coat

Beat well together the eggs, sugar and flavoring. Dip each slice of bread into the mixture to coat both sides. Drain off excess batter and fry in hot oil in a shallow skillet. Brown well on both sides. Drain on paper towels and sprinkle with powdered sugar. You may also wish to pour your favorite syrup over the bread.

When using a griddle as I do, you must spray the bottom with PAM. Allow the griddle to get hot, then cook the bread until brown, flipping it over with a spatula to brown both sides. Serves 1

Couch-couch

(Pronounced "Koosh-koosh")

This was one of my father's favorite dishes to prepare, probably because it was so simple to cook. He sometimes fixed this for supper and then sometimes he would prepare it for breakfast. Regardless of when it was, I really enjoyed it, especially if I had some watermelon rind preserves to add to it.

½   cup oil
2   cups yellow corn meal
1   teaspoon salt
½   teaspoon baking soda
1   teaspoon baking powder
1½ cup water

Heat oil in a heavy skillet. Mix the corn meal, salt, baking soda and baking powder. Add water until it is all moistened and pour into hot skillet. Allow to form a crust before stirring. Stir occasionally after the crust forms. Cover and let cook on low heat for 15 minutes. Serve with milk as a cereal. Top with your favorite preserves. Serves two.

Butterscotch Bread

1 24 ounce package frozen dinner rolls
1 3 ounce Butterscotch pudding mix (not instant)
½ cup brown sugar
½ cup melted butter or margarine
½ cup chopped pecans

Allow rolls to thaw but not rise. Grease a bundt pan well or spray with PAM. Roll dinner rolls in melted butter or margarine. Arrange in bottom of pan to form a layer covering the bottom. Blend pudding mix, brown sugar, and pecans in a small bowl. Sprinkle over rolls. Make layers of rolls and pudding mixture until all rolls and mixture are used. Allow to rise about 1½ hours or until double in bulk. Bake at 350 degrees for 35 minutes. Remove from oven and turn out on a large platter. Serve hot. Serves 6

Second Variation

Vanilla Bread

1 package of 24 frozen dinner rolls
½ cup melted butter or margarine
1 3 ounce vanilla pudding and pie mix—not instant
1 teaspoon cinnamon
½ teaspoon nutmeg
½ cup chopped pecans

Allow rolls to thaw but not rise. Spray bundt pan with PAM or grease well with butter. Arrange rolls which have been rolled in butter or margarine on bottom of pan. Blend pudding mix, cinnamon, nutmeg, and pecans and sprinkle over rolls. Make layers of rolls and pudding mixture until all is used. Allow to rise until double in bulk about 1½ hours. Bake at 350 degrees for 35 minutes. Remove from oven and turn out on large platter. Serve hot.

This smells so good when it comes out of the oven. These two variations were the biggest hit at our recent family reunion. Every one wanted my sister-in-law Carolyn's recipe and I am sure that it will be enjoyed by all again and again.

DRINKS

Rodney Langlenais relaxes with his daughter at the Rock-A-Bye Club in Forked Island after a day of working his cattle.

This is typical of any Cajun family. A Cajun's day usually ends with the enjoyment of family and cool drinks.

DRINKS

Egg Nog Noel

My family never served egg nog. However, the first Christmas Eve at my in-laws' introduced me to this wonderful recipe. My mother-in-law simply whipped up a batch for her family, which numbered about 30. It was great!

1   **dozen separated eggs**
1   **cup sugar**
2½ **pints whipping cream**
1   **quart milk**
1   **cup Southern Comfort**
   Sugar to taste

Separate eggs. Whip whites in a large bowl and add sugar. This mixture should be very stiff and form soft peaks. Beat yolks in another bowl. Whip cream until stiff in another large bowl. Fold egg yolks into whipped whites. Add to whipped cream. Stir in milk. Add Southern Comfort and stir until well blended. Add sugar to your taste if necessary. The whiskey actually cooks the egg yolks. Serves 6.

NOTES

Champagne Punch

3 ripe pineapples
1 pound powdered sugar
1¾ cups lemon juice
½ cup curacao
¾ cup maraschino cherry juice
2 cups brandy
2 cups light rum
4 bottles chilled champagne

Peel, slice and crush pineapple (may be bought already prepared) and place in bottom of large bowl. Cover pineapple and pineapple juice with powdered sugar and allow mixture to stand for 1 hour. Then add fresh lemon juice, curacao, maraschino cherry juice, brandy and light rum. Allow to stand for at least 4 hours in refrigerator. Just before serving, add chilled champagne and ice ring (mold) to bowl and serve.

Ice Ring (Mold)
water
fruit of choice
greenery of choice (I use strawberries and mint leaves)

Decide how large you want the ring to be. Then measure the amount of water to be used by filling the proper mold full of tap water. Set the water aside in another bowl, stirring well 4 or 5 times to allow the air in it to escape and produce clear, pretty ice. Partially freeze a small layer of water, about ½ inch deep in the mold to a slushy consistency. Arrange a wreath of fruit and greenery in the slush and cover carefully with a second layer of very cold water. Return mold to the freezer and add layers as the mold allows. To remove the ring from the mold, turn it upside down and wrap a hot towel around it until the ice is disengaged. Add to the punch bowl when the punch is ready to serve. Serves 20-25.

The old Cajuns did not drink champagne. Their drink of choice was beer (the home-brewed kind). Eventually, they did cultivate a taste for champagne, but only for special occasions such as baptisms, weddings, and birthdays. I recently encountered this punch when I helped one of my daughters host a bridal lingerie shower. Needless to say, everyone went home happy.

A quart of pink lemonade may be added to the punch to weaken it.

Cafe Au Lait

(Coffee Milk)

2   cups milk
1   cup hot or cold coffee
3   tablespoons sugar

Pour coffee into milk. Add sugar and stir well.

Good with French toast or just plain buttered toast for breakfast or simply as a drink, especially on cold days.

I was introduced to this at a very early age (one year old). My parents started every morning with a cup of very strong coffee, and again in the afternoon. I insisted on sharing a cup with them. To pacify me, my mother would pour me a cup of cafe au lait and everyone started their day happy, especially me. I still use a lot of cream and sugar in my coffee, and every morning, I still drink a glass of cafe au lait to renew old memories.

Strawberry Float

1   strawberry soda
2   scoops of ice cream, preferably
    homemade vanilla

Put scoops of ice cream in tall glass. Pour bottle of soda over ice cream and allow to melt a little. Drink with a straw.

This accompanies my grandmother's tomato-sausage recipe. One is not complete without the other.

Mint Julep

2 teaspoons sugar syrup or 1 teaspoon
    powdered sugar
5-6 fresh mint leaves
    dash Angostura bitters
1 ounce fine bourbon whiskey
1 ounce whiskey
16 ounce glass or silver mug
    finely crushed ice to fill glass

Chill serving glass before using. Combine sugar syrup or powdered sugar, bitters and mint leaves. Blend carefully by stirring together. Pour large jigger of whiskey in bar glass and add sugar mixture. Stir again. Remove serving glass from refrigerator, pack it with ice. Strain the above mixture into the glass. With a bar spoon or tea spoon, churn ice up and down. Add more ice to reach within ¾ inch of top of glass. Add the remaining whiskey. Repeat churning process until glass begins to frost. Decorate with a slice of pineapple, orange or lemon and a cherry. Serve with a straw

Our friends from Belgium really enjoyed this new drink. While we were touring with them, we ate supper at a gorgeous southern plantation home. This drink was served before supper and it was delightfully refreshing. It was my first time to experience this drink and I thoroughly enjoyed the whole evening as well as the Mint Julep

Notes

_____

_____

_____

_____

_____

_____

RICE

Harvest time is always the best time of the year and the most exciting!

The crops of the year's hard work are harvested. Members of our family get together and help each other. This is also a means of family unity which is so typical in Cajun life.

The men work hard all day in the fields and the women work hard preparing big, delicious meals for all the hungry mouths. Harry's job usually is to drive his combine (as pictured on the opposite page).

The noon meal is eaten at home, all together then. Supper is partaken of at the camp where everyone relives their day and tries to see who cut the most rice.

The "crew" moves from one field to another until all the crops are harvested.

RICE

Rice

Since I was born and raised on a rice farm and then later became a rice producer myself, it is no surprise that you find this recipe in my section. Rice was served every day at my home and is still served that often. It is prepared along with potatoes and beans or simply covered with good gravy. Rice is economical to prepare and is very versatile. A meal at home isn't complete without it.

I sometimes use a rice cooker, making it easy to cook. Most of the time, however, I prepare it the old way. Regardless, I add 1 teaspoon of vinegar per 3 cups of rice (adding it to the water after it's been measured). This helps the kernels to hold firm and gives them a beautiful white, clean look. The butter or margarine gives it a fuller, richer flavor and keeps it from sticking to the bottom of the pot. Both are really optional.

Another method of cooking rice — one not widely known or seen in cookbooks—is to use a spaghetti cooker or steamer. I started using this method when my husband was diagnosed for diabetes. Removing starch from the diet is best for diabetics since it converts immediately to sugar when in the bloodstream.

Rinse 3 cups of rice in a spaghetti cooker or steamer insert. Replace the insert onto the pot. Add 6 to 8 cups of water and 1 teaspoon of vinegar. Bring to a boil and continue boiling until the kernels double in size (this takes about 15 minutes) and appear done. I usually taste to see if it's done. Then pull the insert out of the pot, drain the starchy water and rinse off the excess starches by putting the insert under a cold water faucet and allowing the water to run through the rice while you stir it. Then replace the insert inside the pot and allow to drain. When ready to serve, reheat the amount needed in a microwave or warm slowly over a low flame. The grains will just roll apart and they taste so good.

Refrigerate all the leftover rice. It will keep for as long as a week if tightly covered, and can be frozen indefinitely.

Other Ways To Prepare Rice

1 cup regular milled long grain rice
2 cups water or other liquid
1 tablespoon butter
Takes 15 minutes.
or
1 cup regular milled medium or short grain rice
1¾ cups water or other liquid
1 tablespoon butter
Takes 15 minutes.
or
1 cup brown rice
2½ cups water or other liquid
1 tablespoon butter
Takes 45-50 minutes.
or
1 cup parboiled rice
2½ cups water or other liquid
1 tablespoon butter
Takes 20-25 minutes.

Combine rice, liquid and butter in 2-3 quart saucepan. Bring to a hard boil. Stir once or twice. Reduce heat, cover and simmer for specified time. If rice is not tender or liquid is not all absorbed, replace lid and cook 2-4 minutes longer. Fluff with fork. Serves 2-3.

Liquids other than water can be used to attain different flavors. Suggestions are chicken or beef stocks, bouillon, consomme, tomato or other vegetable juices, or fruit juice. If juices are used, add one part water to 1 part juice. Recommended juices are apple and orange.

To microwave rice, combine rice, liquid and butter in a 2-3 quart deep microwave baking dish. Cover with an absorbent towel, and cook on high for 5 minutes or until boiling. Reduce heat to medium and cook 15 minutes longer for parboiled rice or 30 minutes longer for brown rice. Fluff with a fork.

Fried Rice with Eggs

My younger daughter submitted a candy recipe to me. However, because I have no candy section (and also because Cajuns seldom make candy), I will use another of her old Cajun rice recipes which I taught her to cook.

1 cup cooked cooled rice
¼ cup oil
2 eggs
   salt and pepper to taste
¼ cup chopped onion tops

Heat skillet with oil. Add cooked rice. Fry until all is hot. Add beaten eggs,salt and pepper and chopped green onion tops. Continue cooking on medium heat until all the eggs are cooked. Serve immediately. Serves one.

Breakfast Rice

1 pound Jimmy Dean Sausage(Sage or Hot)
1 cup chopped onion
1 cup chopped celery
½ cup chopped red bell pepper
½ cup chopped yellow pepper
2 cloves chopped garlic
2 10 ounce cans cream of mushroom soup
1 10 ounce can cream of chicken soup
1 cup raw rice
¼ teaspoon salt
¼ teaspoon pepper
  Louisiana hot sauce to taste(optional)

Brown sausage in a skillet. Drain the grease,remove the sausage and return the grease to the skillet.(If the sausage is too lean,it may be necessary to add one tablespoon of cooking oil to sauté the vegetables). Add the chopped onions,celery,peppers,and garlic. Sauté well. Add the cooked sausage and the soups. Heat thoroughly, making sure all the ingredients are mixed well. Add the rice and the seasonings. Mix. Pour into a casserole sprayed with PAM. Cover and bake at 350 degrees for one hour. Serves 4-6

The Riceland Foods, Inc. annual breakfast committee chairman, Ralph Knapp, asked me to prepare a rich dish for that occasion. Being that Cajuns never ate rice for breakfast, I had to think hard about a good dish. I came up with this idea and it went over very well. Then I also passed it over to a friend, Carl, in Dallas, Texas. He liked it so much that he served it to his entire family for the breakfast meal on Christmas morning. It is so easy, simple and economical to fix. It may even be prepared a day in advance. (To economize, use all green bell peppers and one can of each of the soups and add one can full of water.

Dirty Rice Dressing

Whenever we have a large gathering, rice dressing is always on the menu. The good thing about this dish is that it goes with anything. It also can be used as a main course. I use the left-over dressing, if any, to stuff bell peppers and bake. But it is just as good to just reheat plainly the following day. Children love to eat it. At home we always made rice dressing instead of cornbread dressing. And we still do.

1	pound chicken gizzards, ground
1	pound ground beef or pork
1	cup oil
1	cup chopped onion
½	cup chopped bell pepper
¼	cup chopped celery
	salt and pepper to taste
4	cups cooked rice
¼	cup chopped onion tops

Brown ground meats in oil in a heavy pot. When browned well, add chopped onions, bell pepper and celery. Season to taste. Cook together on a medium heat for 20 minutes. Add rice and onion tops. Mix well, cover and simmer for 10 minutes. Serves 6-8.

The chicken gizzards can be omitted if necessary. Simply use just the beef or pork and cook in the same manner as directed.

Not everyone is lucky enough to live in Cajun Country. Everywhere I go, people say they love my Crawfish Etouffee but can't find any crawfish or they want to make jambalaya and can't find any Andouille. Imagine that!

For that reason, I called some of my friends to see if they could help out. Everyone listed below is accustomed to shipping out their Cajun specialties and other products so that people all over the country can enjoy my Cajun recipes.

Specialty Meats
1123 Forsythe Avenue
Monroe, LA
Phone: 318-324-0888
For: Crawfish tail meat
       Crabmeat
       Oysters

Watkins
17362 Zaunbrecher Road
Jones, LA 71250
Phone: 1-800-361-7102
ID# 78934
For: Vanilla flavoring
       Black Pepper
       Other spices and extracts

Captain Avery, Inc.
3229 Breard Street
Monroe, LA 71201
For all fresh seafood, call:
       318-388-2278

Rouse Enterprises, Inc.
107 Camelia Drive
P. O. Box 5358
Thibodeaux, LA 70302-5358
Phone: 1-800-688-5998
       or 504-447-5998
Fax: 504-447-5563
For: Beef smoked sausage
       Fresh pork sausage
       Andouille
       Pork or turkey tasso
       Boudin
       Crawfish tails
       Crabmeat
       Shrimp, head on, headless,
       or peeled
       Turtle meat (in season)
       Frog legs
       Alligator meat (in season)
       Louisiana red hot sauce

Riceland Rice is available at your local supermarket. If not, please call 1-800-257-5829 for more information.

LE LIVRE EN VISION — TELEVISION
(THE BOOK IN VISION — TELEVISION)

Can you imagine a Cajun with her own television show? I didn't until I decided to do something real daring yet worthwhile. And I love it!!!

I enjoy being with people and talking—and no better way to do that than via television. Besides, one of my friends (and with friends like Blaise, I do not need enemies) told me he really enjoyed my show because that was the only way he could ever turn me off.

Now I can talk to many people plus help preserve my Cajun culture and cooking at the same time.

I thank God (and the General) for allowing me, just a simple Cajun woman, to do what I am doing in conjunction with this cookbook.

Apple Salad

This delicious salad is so simple to make. My daughter, Barbara, showed me how to make it and we all enjoy it now.

4   green apples, cored and sliced
¼   cup finely chopped celery
½   cup golden raisins
¼   cup mayonnaise

Mix all ingredients well and refrigerate overnight. Serves 4.

Pea Salad

This is another great and simple salad. It can be used as a vegetable as well to accompany any meal. So I usually fix this for company or when I am running out of time for fixing my meal. It isn't Cajun of origin but I fix it often.

1   large can early peas, drained
½   medium onion, grated
    salt and pepper to taste
2   boiled eggs, peeled and chopped
½   cup mayonnaise

Grate onion over peas in a bowl. Add rest of ingredients. Mix thoroughly. Refrigerate or serve immediately (better if left standing for a couple of hours). Serves 4.

NOTES

Crawfish or Shrimp Noodle Salad

1 8 ounce bag elbow macaroni, or one 12 ounce bag rotini, cooked
2 pounds crawfish tail meat or 2 cans small cocktail shrimp
2 cups finely chopped bell pepper
2 cups finely chopped celery
1 cup finely chopped onion
1 large can chopped pitted black olives
1 7 ounce jar chopped green olives
6-8 boiled eggs, peeled and chopped
1 pound bacon, fried crisp and crumbled
2 cups mayonnaise (according to taste)
  salt and pepper to taste
1 cup shredded cheese
1 small package Hidden Valley dressing mix

At an Easter family gathering, Cena Mae, one of my sisters-in-law, brought this dish for all of us to enjoy. Since then it has become a regular for my parties, meetings, or simply for my family to enjoy.

Boil macaroni or rotini according to instructions on the package. Rinse with cold water. Drain.

(If you use fresh shrimp or crawfish, boil or sauté them until fully cooked before putting into salad).

Mix all the ingredients very well. Refrigerate for a couple of hours or overnight. Serve with crackers as a dish or on a bed of lettuce as a salad. Serves 6-8.

Bananas Foster

*I made this very often
when my children
were growing up. It is
a fantastic dessert and
will always impress
your company. Now,
of course, thanks to
Chef Hans, I use his
mix as he did…on my
show.*

2 tablespoons butter
¼ cup light brown sugar
1 teaspoon cinnamon
¼ teaspoon lemon peel
4 bananas, peeled and cut in quarters
½ cup dark rum, light rum may be used
¼ cup water

Melt butter in a skillet. Mix brown sugar, cinnamon and lemon peel. Add to melted butter and stir until well blended. Add bananas and rum. Flambé (ignite rum by tipping skillet slightly) and allow alcohol to cook out (the skillet must be very hot and over a high fire to accomplish this). If the mixture is too thick, add water slowly until desired consistency is reached. Serve over vanilla ice cream. Serves 6.

NOTES

GASTON P. BERGERON

My Apple Pie

2 crust pie shell

Line 9-inch pie pan with one crust.

*Apple pie and coffee is
not only "Cajun" but
also "American". It is
so simple to make and
everyone loves it!*

Filling
1½ **cups sugar**
3 **tablespoons flour**
¼ **teaspoon nutmeg**
1 **teaspoon cinnamon**
6 **medium Granny Smith apples,
cored and sliced thin**

Mix all dry ingredients together. Pour over
apples and mix thoroughly. Add the apple mixture into the pie shell. Cover with the second
pie crust. Make four small slits on the top crust.

Glaze
2 **tablespoons sugar**
4 **tablespoons water**

Mix the sugar with water well. Paint the top
crust with this mixture and bake at 375 degrees
for one hour or until golden brown. Cool or
serve warm. May be topped with ice cream.
Serves 6.

Blackberry Dumplings

1 **gallon blackberries, washed**
2½ **cups sugar**
water to cover top of berries

Place berries, sugar and water in a large pot. Bring to a boil and cook on medium heat for about 20-30 minutes.

Dough (can be made while berries cook)
1 **box yellow cake mix**
2 **eggs, beaten**
1 **teaspoon baking powder**
2 **cups water**
2½ **cups flour**

To make dough, blend first four ingredients with an electric mixer. Add flour gradually and mix until the dough is stiff. Knead by hand.

Drop dough by teaspoonfuls into berries that are cooking on simmer. Make sure that the dumplings are far enough apart to allow to rise. Cover and simmer for exactly five minutes. Turn the dumplings over on the other side, cover and simmer for five more minutes. Remove from berries. Cook as much of the dough as needed in the same manner then put the rest in the refrigerator to be used at a later time (may keep for one week). Other types of fruits may be used such as strawberries, peaches or pears—fresh, frozen or canned. To serve, put dumplings in a small bowl, add berries and ice cream (optional). Eat warm or cold.

This is my favorite dessert! I simply love this dish!! Mama always fixed this for me. Now I cook it myself but I am still too afraid of snakes to pick the fresh berries. I buy them by the gallon, wash them, coat them with sugar and freeze them until needed—or I simply buy them in the grocery store already frozen. Of course, my friend Don Dominque waits till he can get the fresh strawberries to make this dish in his restaurant in Monroe.

Heavenly Berries In A Cloud

Meringue layer (crust)
6 **egg whites**
½ **teaspoon salt**
¼ **cup sugar**
1 **teaspoon vanilla**

Beat all the ingredients until very stiff. Pour into a 13x9x2 inch pan (if you wish the crust to be thinner, pour into a larger pan). Bake in preheated 275 degree oven for one hour. Turn the oven off. Leave the pan in oven overnight or until crust is completely cooled.

This is a new dessert that I recently learned how to fix. It was one of the dishes at a 4-H rice cookery contest that I judged. It is gorgeous and very, very delicious!

Rice layer
1 **cup whipping cream**
4 **ounces cream cheese**
½ **cup sugar**
1 **cup miniature marshmallows**
2 **cups cooked and cooled rice**

In the morning, or when ready to prepare dish, beat whipping cream until stiff. In another bowl, mix cream cheese and sugar. Set aside.

Add marshmallows to whipping cream that has been beaten. Fold in rice. Fold whipping cream mixture into cream cheese mixture. Spread over the meringue shell leaving 1 inch of shell showing on all sides.

Topping
1 **can dark Bing cherries**
1 **cup sugar**
2 **tablespoons cornstarch**

Cook the above until thickened. You may use any canned pie filling instead of the cherries. Pour this topping over the rice layer. Refrigerate for one hour or overnight before serving. Serves 8.

Smothered Cabbage

My parents loved cabbage but I didn't— until I tried this dish. Now, this is one of my favorites! I guarantee this will be enjoyed by anyone (it even smells good).

1   **medium head of cabbage, cored and chopped**
5   **slices of bacon**
    salt and pepper to taste

Fry bacon in heavy pot. Add chopped cabbage. Cover. Stir occasionally (cabbage will brown in bacon drippings as the two cook together). Cook for about 30 minutes. Salt and pepper to taste. Serve hot. Serves 4-6.

Mardi Gras Salad Dressing Mix

Cajuns do not have many different salad dressings. This is one I just recently threw together. Umm, umm! Good!

1   **cup cider vinegar**
½   **cup oil**
1   **teaspoon dry mustard**
½   **cup sugar**
½   **cup finely chopped onion**
    salt and pepper to taste

Mix all the dressing ingredients in a blender (or a jar). Blend well and pour over vegetables such as lettuce, tomato, cucumber, etc. Toss. Serve immediately. Serves 6.

Carrot Salad

1½ cups shredded carrots
1   cup coconut
2   tablespoons lemon juice
¼   cup raisins (I prefer the golden raisins)
½   teaspoon ground ginger
¼   cup cut-up pineapple
1   cup mayonnaise (may use more or less, according to taste)

Mix all the ingredients thoroughly. Chill. Serves 4.

Mama did not like carrots, so we never had this salad at home. But as I ventured off and tried new dishes, I learned to like carrots (she never did, however). Even one of my friends, Chris, who does not like coconut or raisins is very fond of this salad.

Smothered Squash

6   medium yellow or white squash, washed and chopped (if using white squash, peel, but it is not necessary to peel yellow squash)
1   medium size onion, sliced thin
2   tablespoons butter
2   tablespoons sugar
¼   cup water
    salt and pepper to taste

Cook squash, onion and butter on medium heat until squash is real tender. Stir occasionally. Season to taste. Mash with a potato masher, pastry blender or a fork. Add sugar. Mix well. Serves 4-6.

We had this real often when I was growing up. Then I introduced it to the General and our children. Barbara especially likes this dish.

Stuffed Shrimp
à Chef Hans

Chef Hans has taught me a lot about cooking, especially about Creole cooking. And I must admit that his Creole cooking is as good as my Cajun cooking! This is one of his many specialties that I enjoy preparing for my family or for special company.

16   large shrimp, peeled, deveined and butterflied
½   stick butter
¼   cup onion, chopped fine
½   cup flour
1   cup water or chicken broth
¼   cup finely chopped celery
¼   cup finely chopped parsley
    salt and pepper to taste
1   pound lump crabmeat
¼   cup melted butter
½   cup breadcrumbs
2   tablespoons white wine
½   cup sherry
    salt and pepper—or use Creole seasoning

Peel each shrimp, leaving the tail attached. Take a small knife and cut down the center of the bottom of the shrimp. Remove the feedline (vein). Set aside laying the shrimp in a baking dish that has been lined with oil or sprayed with Pam.

Melt butter in another saucepan. Sauté the onions in the butter. Add flour and blend until like coarse cornmeal. Add water or chicken broth. Mix well until creamy. Add celery and parsley. Season to taste. Mix well. Fold in crabmeat.

Continued on next page

Mix melted butter and breadcrumbs. Set aside.

Take a tablespoon of stuffing and place over shrimp. Sprinkle the breadcrumbs over the stuffing. Pull the shrimp's tail over the stuffing. Bake at 350 degrees for 20-25 minutes or until the shrimp is done, depending on the size of the shrimp. Pour wine and sherry over shrimp just before serving.

This stuffing can also be used in preparation of other dishes.

NOTES

"Z" Sausage

This is a family recipe—the Zaunbrechers have made this for many, many years. It was a big deal to butcher hogs and make sausage, boudin and hogshead cheese for us to enjoy at Christmas. So in honor of the Zaunbrecher tradition (and also because Dr. Logan Gardiner requested it) I have included this recipe. ENJOY!

1 pound coarsely ground beef
3 pounds coarsely ground pork
salt and pepper to taste
red pepper to taste
1 teaspoon curing salt (optional)
¼ cup sugar
1 tablespoon nutmeg
1 pint boiling water
3 heads garlic, peeled
casings to stuff all meat—may be purchased at slaughter house or at meat market

Season the ground meats. Mix well. Add sugar and nutmeg. Mix well.

To make the garlic juice, put garlic in a jar. Pour the boiling water over garlic and allow to stand for at least three hours. Take out garlic. Use about ½ cup of the garlic juice. Add to mixture of meat. Mix well.

Put meat in sausage maker and fill the casings until all the meat is used. Tie the ends of the links, using a short string or thread.

To cook, lay the sausage links in a heavy skillet with about ¾ cup of water all allow to cook slowly until done. Turn the sausage over on the other side and allow to brown slowly on both sides. Be careful not to break the casing when browning or turning over. Add more water if necessary.

Continued on next page

Classic
CAJUN

You may not wish to stuff sausage in a casing but to only make sausage patties. If so, simply form the patties same as hamburger patties and fry in a heavy skillet on a medium heat until done (about 30 minutes).

This can be a meal or served with eggs and biscuits for breakfast. Makes about six twelve inch links or 10 patties.

NOTES

Rice Fruit Cocktail Salad

This is a dish that my parents would not have liked because they serve rice with gravy at meals, not as a dessert or a salad. However I have served this at the Agricultural/Business Esposition in Monroe for at least twelve years. It is surprisingly delicious!

1   8 ounce package cream cheese
3   tablespoons sugar
1½ tablespoons mayonnaise
1   cup cool whip
1   small can crushed pineapple, drained
1   large can fruit cocktail, drained
½   cup finely chopped pecans
2   cups cooked and cooled rice
1   6 ounce package small marshmallows
    cherries to decorate

Cream together cream cheese, sugar, mayonnaise, and cool whip. Add the rest of the ingredients and mix thoroughly. Refrigerate. This may also be served as a dessert. Serves 6.

Janet's Sherry Fruit Salad

This is a big hit at our camp suppers and also around the holidays. My sister-in-law Janet and I particularly like it!

3   oranges, peeled and sliced
3   apples, peeled and sliced thin or chopped up
3   bananas, peeled and sliced
¼   cup lemon juice
1   cup coconut
1   cup cherry juice
1   small jar cherries
1   cup seedless golden raisins
¼   cup sugar or 1 package Nutra-sweet
¾   cup sherry

Mix all the above ingredients together well. Allow to stand in refrigerator overnight. Serves 6.

Harvey Wallbanger Cake

1   **box orange cake mix**
1   **3-3¾ ounce package instant vanilla
    pudding mix**
¾   **cup orange juice**
½   **cup oil**
4   **eggs**
¼   **cup vodka**
¼   **cup Galliano**

In a large mixing bowl, combine all ingredients.
Beat for 4 minutes on medium with electric
mixer. Pour into baking pans which you've
sprayed with nonstick coating. Bake for 35
minutes at 350 degrees. Glaze while warm.

Glaze

1   **cup sugar**
1   **tablespoon orange juice**
1   **tablespoon vodka**
1   **tablespoon Galliano**
1   **tablespoon white corn syrup**

Combine ingredients in a small bowl. Stir until
smooth, and drizzle over warm cake.

*This is a wonderful
cake! It is all so easy
to make. And it's
always the hit of the
party. To make it
pretty, I usually bake
it in a baking ring or
bundt pan.*

Chess Pie

1   **cup sugar**
2   **egg yolks**
½   **cup whipping cream**
¼   **cup butter, melted**
2   **tablespoons cornmeal**
1   **teaspoon Watkin's vanilla flavoring**

Beat sugar and eggs. Add cream and melted
butter. Add cornmeal and vanilla. Beat well.
Pour in unbaked pie shell. Bake for 45 minutes
at 350 degrees. Serves 6.

*I was shocked when I
learned that this pie
had cornmeal in it. A
wonderful neighbor,
Erie Brown, who
helped me a lot when I
first moved to North
Louisiana, gave me this
recipe. It is most un-
Cajun but most tasty!*

Laura Bess's Special Carrot Cake

Our very dear friends, Harold and Beverly McCormack, from Memphis, Tennessee, came to visit us recently. They used to live near us and always loved to visit and enjoy my cooking, especially Doc. And, of course, I love to cook for them—usually crawfish since I was the first to introduce them to the little critters. Doc shared this special recipe with me saying that this was his daughter Laura Bess's specialty. The cake is truly very special as so is she!

2	cups sugar
4	eggs, beaten
1¼	cups oil
2	teaspoons Watkin's vanilla flavoring
2¼	cups flour
2	teaspoons cinnamon
¼	teaspoon nutmeg, freshly ground
¼	teaspoon allspice
2	teaspoons baking soda
1	teaspoon salt
2	cups shredded carrots
2	cups coconut
8	ounces crushed pineapple
1	cup pecans, chopped
1	cup raisins

In a large mixing bowl, beat sugar and eggs until creamy. Add oil and vanilla and mix thoroughly. In another bowl, mix flour, cinnamon, nutmeg, allspice, baking soda and salt. Add to beaten egg mixture. Mix well. Add carrots, coconut, pineapple, pecans and raisins and mix well.

Pour batter in three 8 inch round baking pans which have been sprayed with nonstick coating. Bake at 350 degrees for 50-60 minutes or until well done. (To test, insert a toothpick in center of layers. If it comes out clean, the cake is done). Do not overbake.

(Continued on next page)

(Laura Bess's Special Carrot Cake continued)

Icing

1 12 ounce package Philadelphia cream cheese
1 teaspoon Watkin's vanilla flavoring
¼ cup milk
3-4 cups powdered sugar

Beat Philadelphia cream cheese with vanilla and milk until smooth. Add enough powdered sugar till it reaches spreading consistency.

Creamy Banana Pudding

1 14 ounce can sweetened condensed milk
1½ cups cold milk
1 4 serving size package instant vanilla flavor or butterscotch flavor pudding mix
2 cups (1 pint) whipping cream, whipped
36 vanilla wafers
3 medium bananas, sliced

In a large bowl, combine condensed milk, milk and pudding mix; beat well. Chill 5 minutes. Fold in whipped cream. In a serving bowl, layer the bottom with wafers, bananas and pudding. Continue to layer till all is used. Top with Cool Whip or whipped cream. Refrigerate.

This was something we often had at home after my brother Keith decided this was his favorite dish. Mama was not a dessert maker, but she made sure Keith had this at least once a week. Not to mention that I was pretty fond of it myself.

Momo Ding's Pecan Pralines

A very good friend of mine, Yvette Waller, submitted this recipe to me. She is another Cajun girl with deep Cajun roots. She's a lovely person and I feel honored to know her and put her grandmother's praline recipe in my cookbook.

5   cups white sugar
5   cups pecans, broken
1   can sweetened condensed milk
1   cup Pet milk
1   teaspoon salt
1   block butter or margarine
2   teaspoons vanilla

Spread the table with section thick newspaper and cover with waxed paper.

Mix sugar, pecans, milk, and salt. Cook on medium fire, stirring *constantly* until sugar dissolves. Cook to hard ball stage. Momo Ding always said you had to cook it till it looked like red beans. You could tell it was ready by dripping some into a cup of cold water—if it made a hard ball, it was ready.

Remove from heat and add butter and vanilla. Beat until it loses shine and leaves the spoon. Drop quickly. Makes about 4 dozen.

Momo Ding (Elaine Rodriquez) and Mom (Myra Waller) always made a double batch of these in the Magnalite Dutch Oven. They always said you had to have two people to do a double batch, but if more than two tried to drop the pralines, someone would get burned. I watched them make pralines every year at Christmas time as I was growing up. The year my grandmother died, Mom asked if I thought I could help her make the pralines—she didn't want the tradition to end. I said that of course I could help. I had watched them make pralines so many times I was sure I'd have no problem helping. It was a lot of work, but the pralines were delicious and I felt closer to Mom that year than I had ever felt before.

(Momo Ding's Pecan Pralines continued)

This year (1996), my aunt was at Mom's when we made the pralines. All three of us were dropping pralines at the same time. We joked that Momo Ding always said more than two could not drop at the same time or someone would get burned. Yet here we were, all three dipping our spoons into the pot and banging them on the counter—it sounded like a bunch of woodpeckers. One time when I was dipping my spoon into the pot, Aunt Susie hit my knuckles with her spoon. I jumped—more out of fear than pain—and said, "I guess that was Momo Ding's way of telling us 'I told you so!'"

Chocolate Pie à Dale

1   **cup sugar, divided**
3   **tablespoons cornstarch**
1   **teaspoon Hershey's cocoa**
⅛   **teaspoon salt**
3   **cups milk**
3   **eggs, separated**
1   **tablespoon butter**
1   **teaspoon Watkin's vanilla flavoring**

This is a very unusual chocolate pie being that it has very little cocoa in it. Dale and Sylvia Ross gave me this recipe and I love it!

Mix sugar, cornstarch, cocoa, and salt together. Add to heated milk and whisk till all blended. Cook till it starts to thicken. Beat egg yolks, add to mixture and cook till thick. Remove from heat. Add butter and vanilla; allow to cool. Pour into baked 9 inch pie shell. Beat 3 egg whites and ¼ cup sugar to form meringue and cover pie. Allow to bake at 400 degrees for 10 minutes. Allow to cool completely.

Sweet Potato Pie

I got to be real good
friends with Edwina
Harper from Bonita.
She and I both were
active in the Farm
Bureau Women's
Committee. I
promoted rice as a
commodity and she
promoted sweet
potatoes. To me, her
sweet potato pie was
the best I ever ate.

3 eggs, separated
1 cup sugar, divided
1 cup cooked mashed sweet potatoes
1 teaspoon ground cinnamon
1 teaspoon ground pumpkin pie spice
½ teaspoon ground nutmeg
½ cup milk
1 tablespoon unflavored gelatin
¼ cup cold water
1 baked 9 inch pastry shell

Beat egg yolks until thick and lemon colored in top of a double boiler. Add ½ cup sugar, sweet potatoes, spices and milk. Soften gelatin in ¼ cup cold water. Cook potato mixture in top of double boiler, stirring constantly, until thick. When thick, stir in softened gelatin until dissolved. Let cool 10 minutes. Beat egg whites until stiff, adding remaining ½ cup sugar. Fold egg whites into cooled potato mixture. Pour into baked pie shell. Chill 2 hours. Yield: one 9 inch pie.

Pie Crust
1 cup all-purpose flour
¼ cup firmly packed brown sugar
½ cup butter, softened
½ cup chopped pecans

Combine flour and sugar; cut in butter until mixture resembles coarse crumbs. Stir in pecans. Press mixture firmly into a 9 inch pan. Bake at 400 degrees for 15 minutes or until golden brown. While pastry is hot, break up pie shell and press evenly into pie pan once again, if desired. Yield: one 9 inch pie shell.

Classic White Chocolate Bread Pudding

Since I am a chocoholic, I deeply love this bread pudding. It is so good, it's sinful. I just recently started making this and introducing it to all my family and friends. Look out arteries, here it comes!

- 6 **cups whipping cream**
- 2 **cups milk**
- 1 **cup sugar**
- 1 **teaspoon grated nutmeg**
- 20 **ounces white chocolate (kisses)**
- 4 **whole eggs**
- 13 **egg yolks**
- 1 **24 inch loaf French bread, sliced**
  ¾ inch thick, or enough stale bread
  to cover pan

Preheat the oven to 350 degrees.

In a large saucepan, beat the whipping cream, milk, sugar and nutmeg over medium heat. When hot, take off heat and add white chocolate pieces. Stir until melted.

Combine the whole eggs and egg yolks in a large bowl. Slowly pour the hot cream mixture into the eggs, whipping as you pour.

Put the sliced bread in the pan. Pour ½ the bread pudding mix over the bread. Press the bread down with your hands until it absorbs the liquid and becomes soggy. Pour in the remaining mix.

Cover the pan with foil and bake in oven for 1 hour. Take off the foil and bake for an additional ½ hour or until it is set and golden brown.

White Chocolate Sauce
- 8 **ounces white chocolate pieces**
- ½ **cup whipping cream**

Bring the cream to a slow boil in a small saucepan. Take off the heat and add the white chocolate. Stir until completely melted. Spoon over the bread pudding. Serves 12.

Custard Pie

2½   cups heated milk
4   eggs, beaten
1   cup sugar
¾   stick margarine
1   teaspoon Watkin's vanilla flavoring

Heat milk. Beat eggs. Add sugar to eggs and beat again. Pour hot milk into egg mixture. Put mixture back into pot. Add margarine. Heat very hot but do not boil. Take off heat and add vanilla. Pour into uncooked pie shell. Bake at 350 degrees for about 30 minutes or just until the custard is not quite set. (Shake the pie to see when it is almost set). Remove from oven and set aside till cooled or just set—this is real good warm. Serves 6.

I'll never forget the first time I tried baking this pie. I didn't have any other ingredients at hand so I decided this may be real good. And it was! It was quick and easy in a big emergency. Dale and Sylvia also couldn't believe it was my first try at custard pie.

"Cat Heads"

(REDNECK BISCUITS)

2   cups flour
3   teaspoons baking powder
1   teaspoon salt
⅓   cup Crisco
¾   cup milk

Mix flour, baking powder and salt in a mixing bowl. Cut Crisco into flour mixture with pastry blender or with two knives until mixture looks like coarse cornmeal. Add milk and stir just enough to hold dough together. Put dough on floured board and knead lightly a few times. Roll dough ¼ to ½ inch thick. Cut with large biscuit cutter or large opened mouth jar dipped in flour before each cutting. Place biscuits, separated, on ungreased cookie sheet; bake in hot oven at 425 degrees for 12-15 minutes or until brown as desired.

I was shocked when a friend of mine said he had eaten "cat heads" for breakfast. From Gueydan, I had never heard of such things (another culture shock). But in Jones, these are well known. I was relieved when my friend explained that "cat heads" were simply large biscuits. So now, I make "cat heads," but mine are usually out of a Pillsbury Grands can.

Sour Cream Pound Cake

3 **cups sugar**
3 **sticks butter**
6 **eggs, separated**
½ **teaspoon salt**
3 **cups flour**
¼ **teaspoon soda**
1 **teaspoon Watkin's vanilla flavoring**
½ **pint sour cream**

Cream together the sugar and butter. Add egg yolks one at a time to creamed mixture. In another bowl, mix salt, flour and soda. Lay aside in another bowl, mix vanilla and sour cream. Add flour mixture and sour cream mixture alternately to creamed mixture. Beat egg whites till very stiff. Fold in the beaten egg whites to the other ingredients which have been mixed all together.

Grease a tube pan. Dust with flour and add cake mixture to pan. Bake for 1¾ hours at 300 degrees. Turn out immediately on wax paper.

This is one of the most delicious sour cream cakes I have ever made. The recipe was handed down to me by Mrs. Gennie Bell Crossley who ended up being my second Mom and best friend in Jones. She lived next door to me when I first moved to Jones. Without her, I do not think I would have survived because, as Shirley Leonards tells it about me, "Lucy would cry once a day all day long when she moved to Jones." And that was true. But Mrs. Gennie Bell took me and my son Todd in like we were her family. I can vividly vision the gorgeous strawberry patch and the good times we shared. Also her husband, Mr. Harry, who checked on me and Todd daily (maybe it was for the cold beer he drank at my house) and always left chewing gum so Mrs. Gennie Bell could not smell the beer. They were a precious couple.

Bouille

½ gallon milk
2 12 ounce cans evaporated milk
6 eggs
1½ cups sugar
1 tablespoon Watkins vanilla flavoring
1 tablespoon Watkins almond flavoring
4 tablespoons cornstarch
¼ cup water
1 angel food cake, sliced in 3 layers
¼ cup whipped topping

This bouille is an old Cajun tradition from my grandmother. We ate this right after she cooked it while it was still warm. Now, I've dressed it up and added the Angel Food Cake. No matter whether Baby Lucy eats it just plain or with the cake, now my granddaughter enjoys this recipe.

I want to dedicate this recipe to Courtney Albritton from West Monroe. A fine young lady who entered it in the District Egg Cookery Contest— and won!

In a 4 quart saucepan, bring milk and evaporated milk to a boil; reduce heat. Beat eggs, sugar and extracts. Dissolve cornstarch in water. Add cornstarch to egg mixture. Gradually add this mixture to the milk, stirring constantly until mixture begins to slightly thicken. Layer in trifle bowl. Begin with cake, bouille, cake, bouille, cake, ending with bouille. Top with whipped topping. Garnish with chocolate syrup, almonds, cherries and/or mint leaves. Serves 6-8.

NOTES

Crème Brûlée

12	vanilla caramels
2¼	cups milk, divided
4	eggs
⅓	cup sugar (optional)
¼	teaspoon salt

Heat caramels and ¼ cup milk in saucepan till they melt, stirring occasionally. Spoon mixture into the bottom of an 8 inch flan pan or divide among six 6 ounce custard cups. Set the dish or cups in a shallow baking pan.

Custard: Heat remaining 2 cups milk. Beat eggs with sugar (optional); add salt. Add to heated milk and mix well. Pour into baking dish.

Place pan on oven rack. Pour hot water into pan to depth of 1 inch. Bake at 350 degrees for 30 minutes. Serve cool or chilled. Just before serving, invert onto dessert plates.

In France, a caramel-sauced baked custard is called crème brûlée; in Spain, it's flan. No matter where you're at, even in Cajun Country now, this is a very special dessert. It is also very impressive.

NOTES

Fruit Cocktail Cake

This wonderful cake recipe was given to me by Julia Wooks from Bonita. I fell in love with it because it was so moist and unusual in taste. Plus it is quick and easy.

2 eggs
1½ cups sugar
1 tablespoon oil
2 cups flour
1 teaspoon soda
½ teaspoon salt
2 15 ounce cans fruit cocktail plus juice
½ cup light brown sugar
¼ cup nuts, chopped

Cream eggs and sugar. Add oil and mix. Sift flour, soda and salt together. Combine mixtures. Beat well. Add fruit cocktail—use juice accordingly. Pour into sheath pan which has been sprayed with a nonstick coating. Sprinkle with brown sugar and chopped nut mixture over top of batter. Bake 30 minutes or until done at 325 degrees.

Icing

¾ cup sugar
1 3½ ounce can coconut
1 stick butter

Cook in saucepan for at least 2 minutes or until butter is all melted. Pour over hot cake. Enjoy!

The Micky

(A POWERFUL, TRANQUILIZING DRINK—

NOT FOR TEE-TOTALERS)

Peaches, fresh and unpeeled
1 **fifth vodka**
1½ **cups sugar**

In a wide mouth gallon jar, drop enough peaches to fill ½ full. If a wide mouth jar is not available, halve the peaches and fill a regular mouth sized jar.

Pour vodka over peaches, add sugar on top. Allow to set, stirring occasionally, for three months. Then, enjoy the peaches as well as the juice! Any fresh fruit may be used to make this drink.

I recall when my parents made their first batch of home brew. It was a disaster!! They were so sick they really didn't care if they ever drank any more beer. (Maybe they just drank too much).

A friend of mine, Micky, gave me this recipe as we were discussing how Cajuns used to make their own beer. He says he prefers this to homemade beer and I can see why. His only problem, he says, is that he can never allow it to set much longer than a couple weeks before he starts sampling. So I dedicate this recipe to him!

Hog's Head Cheese

Enjoy! This is an old German recipe from Mrs. Marie Humble of Gueydan. She would always bring this to Jones when she visited her daughter, Salley, who happened to have been born and raised in Gueydan and ended up being my next door neighbor in Jones.

3-4 **pounds fresh pigs feet**
5 **pounds pork meat, cut in chunks**
   salt and pepper to taste
3 **cloves garlic, finely chopped**
2 **cups green onions, finely chopped**
1 **cup parsley, finely chopped**

Season pork meat. Boil in pot with water and garlic. Put about one inch or so over the meat until the meat is tender (cooked). This takes about 3 to 4 hours. Take out pork. Remove all meat from bones and grind *coarsely*. Add green onions and parsley to the liquid. Pour into pans or molds at least 2 inches deep. Cover with foil, Saran Wrap or plate and put heavy weights on the meat, pressing down. All to cool, then refrigerate overnight. Slice as needed.

Macaroni Salad

This is one of my favorite salads. Even the General, who doesn't like pasta, likes it. I used to fix "tons" of this for harvest crew meals. It is another dish that is better the day after it is made.

1 **16 ounce package elbow macaroni**
1 **6 ounce can small shrimp**
1 **small onion, grated**
   salt and pepper to taste
¼-½ **cup mayonnaise (to taste)**

Boil macaroni according to instructions on package. Rinse. Cool. Drain the shrimp. Add to macaroni. Grate onion over macaroni and shrimp. Season to taste. Add mayonnaise and mix thoroughly. Refrigerate. Serves 6.

New Orleans Onion Soup

ONE OF THE BEST LIKED SOUPS THAT WE
SERVED FOR BRUNCH AT BRENNAN'S AND IT
DOESN'T TAKE TOO MUCH EFFORT TO
PREPARE.

*This is one of Chef
Hans' easy yet
delicious soups. I have
learned to make this
for very special
occasions. This is
another Creole dish.*

½   **stick butter**
2   **medium onions, finely sliced**
⅓   **cup sifted flour**
3   **cups water**
1   **chicken bouillon cube**
1   **ounce dry white wine**
½   **cup shredded cheese**
1   **ounce dry sherry**
     pinch of ground bay leaf
     salt and pepper to taste

Put soup pot on medium heat and melt butter
and onion and stir until tender. Add flour and
combine. Pour in water and bouillon. Stir with
whisk and simmer for 15 minutes. Add wine,
cheese, sherry and seasoning. Stir until cheese
is melted. Tastes great with croutons.

NOTES

Crawfish in Heaven

Ordinarily a main dish for elegant occasions such as weddings, it also makes a good appetizer. But I most often cook it for a family meal. Delicious!! This is another one of Chef Hans' hand-me-down recipes. I have learned a lot from him, but I'll never be the Chef he is!

2 tablespoons butter
1 cup onions, finely chopped
2 tablespoons flour
2 cups milk
1 pound cooked crawfish tails or shrimp
¼ cup half and half cream
½ cup green onions, finely chopped
½ cup parsley, finely chopped
 salt and pepper to taste
2 ounces dry white wine
1 ounce sherry
 red hot sauce to taste
8 ounces cooked angel hair (very, very thin) pasta
1 sprig parsley
1 lemon, thinly sliced
1 whole crawfish, cooked

Melt butter in saucepan over medium heat. Add onions and cook until tender. Add flour, stirring continuously with a wooden spoon for 2 minutes. Using wire whisk, slowly add milk and simmer for 5 to 10 minutes on low heat. Combine crawfish tails (or shrimp) with half and half, then fold into sauce. Add green onions, parsley, seasonings, wine, sherry, and hot sauce to taste. Serve over angel hair pasta. Decorate with cooked whole crawfish, parsley and lemon slices.

Gumbo Verte (Green Gumbo) or Gumbo Z'Herbes (Grass Gumbo)

1   10 ounce package frozen spinach
1   10 ounce package frozen mustard greens
1   10 ounce package frozen turnip tops
1   small head fresh cabbage, cut up ½'s
½   cup cooking oil
½   cup flour
1   cup onion, chopped
½   cup celery, chopped
4   cloves garlic, minced
1   pound shrimp, peeled and deveined
    salt and pepper to taste

Chop all greens well and boil in water. (Better if boiled separately because some vegetables boil faster than others). Drain. Keep all liquids.

Make roux with oil and flour. Brown until medium brown (chocolate). Add the reserved liquid until desired consistency is obtained (like a regular gumbo). Add boiled greens, onion, celery, garlic and salt and pepper. Cook over medium heat until mixture is creamy, about 30 minutes. Serve over rice. Serves 4-6.

Several people have asked me if I had a gumbo verte recipe. Honestly, I didn't because my mama never cooked this. Matter of fact, I had never heard of it before. But it got my curiosity aroused, so I got ideas from several people and came up with this recipe. Needless to say this is not one of my favorites. But I hope you can enjoy it.

Green Gumbo II

No Roux!

20-25 **ounces of any kind of greens**
water
1 **large hen, cut up in serving pieces**
salt and pepper to taste

This is another gumbo verte recipe. It was given to me by Mr. Lee Schexnayder from below Baton Rouge. Mr. Lee always had a wonderful garden and is a great cook. He says the juice of this gumbo is fit for a king.

Boil the greens first. Then drain, reserving juice. Grind or cut up the greens as desired. Put hen in a large gumbo pot, add the greens' juices and enough water extra to boil hen until almost done. Add all the greens and salt and pepper to taste. Cook over medium high heat until hen is completely done (about 20-30 minutes). Serve over rice. Serves 6.

Ricardo's Layered Salad

lettuce
chips
1 **small jar bean dip**
1 **1¼ ounce package taco seasoning**
1 **7 ounce jar guacamole dip or**
1 fresh avocado mashed with
1 teaspoon fresh lemon juice
1 **pint sour cream**
1 **jar salsa, strained**
grated cheddar cheese

For one of my shows, I needed an outstanding salad. So Barbara suggested I use her layered salad recipe which she makes. It was a hit with the camera crew, and since my salad is from a South of the Border origin, I named it Ricardo's Salad in honor of Ricardo, the gentleman who does a wonderful job of editing my show.

In a casserole or deep dish, line bottom of casserole or dish with lettuce leaves. On sides of dish, stand up chips till surrounded. Layer the bean dip; sprinkle taco seasoning over bean dip. Top with guacamole dip or fresh avocado which has been peeled and mashed with fresh lemon juice. Cover with sour cream. Add salsa. Sprinkle grated cheddar cheese over casserole. Serve with remaining chips as dip or use as a great salad.

My Favorite Fruit Salad

2 eggs, beaten
½ cup sugar
⅛ teaspoon dry mustard
⅛ teaspoon salt
juice of 1 medium lemon
1 15¼ ounce can fruit cocktail, drained
½ 6¼ ounce package miniature marshmallows
2 medium bananas, sliced
½ pint whipped cream

This is my favorite fruit salad. I really can't remember where I got this recipe but I did get it many years ago. It's so creamy and smooth that I just eat it anytime during the day and also with my meals.

Beat eggs, sugar, dry mustard and salt well. Add lemon juice. Cook over low heat till it thickens. Remove from heat. Pour drained fruit cocktail in a large bowl. Add marshmallows and bananas or whatever other fresh fruit desired. Whip cream and add to bowl. Mix thoroughly. Then pour the thickened sauce over all ingredients and fold till thoroughly blended. Serves 4-6.

NOTES

Barbecued Shrimp

This is another great recipe which my friend Chef Hans has handed down to me. To me, he is the Master Chef of all chefs! In case you do not have his seasoning, use salt, pepper, cayenne, onion powder, herbs and various spices which you desire. Regardless, it is very tasty.

1	stick butter
½	cup olive oil
½	cup onions, finely chopped
½	cup garlic, finely chopped
1½	ounces Worcestershire sauce
½	cup lemon juice
1	tablespoon Chef Hans' Creole Seasoning
1	tablespoon Chef Hans' Blackened Fish Seasoning
	hot sauce to taste
2	pounds large shrimp, peeled

Preheat oven to 350 degrees. In saucepan, melt butter over medium heat. Add all other ingredients except shrimp and bring to simmer. Place shrimp on baking pan or Pyrex dish then pour butter mixture over shrimp evenly. Bake shrimp for 5 minutes, then turn and cook for a few minutes more until done. Remove from oven and place shrimp and sauce in small bowls. Add Chef Hans' Hot Sauce to taste. Serve with crisp French bread.

NOTES

Fried Frog Legs

8   **frog legs**
    salt and pepper to taste
2½ **cups milk**
2   **eggs, beaten**
    flour
    oil for frying

Season frog legs with salt and pepper. Soak in milk for at least 2 hours. Take out of milk and run through eggs. Then dredge frog legs through flour till well coated. Drop in enough oil for deep frying which has been heated to 400 degrees then reduced to 375 degrees after the frog legs are put in till fried to a golden brown (about 6 minutes). Serves 4-6.

Fried frog legs were mama's favorite dish. Daddy used to go frogging in the canals by the house. Then he'd bring them home in a rice sack, leave them in a cool wet place till the next morning. Then he'd skin them and bring them inside for mama to cook. I, myself, love fried frog legs even though they are real weird when some of them actually seem to "jump" after putting them in the hot oil.

Crawfish Stew

¼   **cup oil**
¼   **cup flour**
1   **pint water**
1   **pound crawfish tail meat**
    salt and pepper to taste
½   **cup green onion tops, chopped**

Make a dark roux with oil and flour. Add water. Bring to a slow boil and boil for about 20-30 minutes. Add crawfish tails, seasoning and onion tops. Cook for about 10-15 minutes until crawfish tails are done. If gravy is too thick, add a little water till it reaches the right consistency. Serve over rice. Serves 3.

I wish I had a dollar for every time Mama cooked this. It was Daddy's favorite crawfish dish. Now it's the General's favorite.

Shrimp Stuffed Bell Peppers

Shrimp and bell pepper really go well together. I sometimes even add boiled or sautéed eggplant to this stuffing for variation. Regardless of what you put in it, it's a gourmet meal in one shell. To make this more interesting, I sometimes not only use bell peppers to stuff, but use eggplants which I've cut out some of the pulp and also put in the stuffing. Then I stuff the eggplant "boot" and bake the same. Talk about good!

1 pound shrimp, peeled and deveined
½ stick butter
½ cup onion, chopped
½ cup bell pepper, chopped
salt and pepper to taste
2 eggs, beaten
1 cup bread crumbs or 4 slices of bread, run though water and squeezed
6-7 bell peppers, tops removed

Sauté shrimp in butter till pink in color and most water cooked out. Add onion and bell pepper and cook for about 10 more minutes, adding dabs of water to prevent sticking. Add seasoning. Let cool. Add eggs and stir well. Add bread crumbs or squeezed bread and mix thoroughly. Stuff into uncooked bell peppers with the tops removed. Lay in a pan which has half of it covered with water. Bake at 350 degrees for 20-30 minutes. Serves 6-7.

General's Broiled Fish

5 catfish fillets
    salt, pepper and Louisiana Red Hot
    sauce to taste
2 garlic cloves, minced
½ medium onion, sliced
3 sprigs celery, sliced in strips
    fresh lemon juice

Line baking pan with foil. Spray with nonstick coating. Layer the seasoned fillets on bottom of pan. Sprinkle garlic over fish. Put slices of onions and strips of celery over garlic. Sprinkle fresh lemon juice over all. Put pan on lowest level of oven and broil fish for 20 minutes. Serve hot. Serves 2.

This is a miracle! The General has finally learned how to cook something! To my amazement, he put this together all by himself one day while I was taking care of one of my daughters. He was so proud that he insisted he'd cook this for me for a meal. And it really is good! I really do not care for broiled or baked fish but I like this! Has a great flavor. Seems I'll be fixing this often.

NOTES

Corn-Crabmeat Chowder

I never had this as I was growing up but now it has become one of my favorites. How can you go wrong with the best seafood and the best vegetable mixed together?

3 tablespoons margarine
1 large onion, chopped
1 medium bell pepper, finely chopped
1 pound crabmeat
1 10¾ ounce can cream of mushroom soup
1 15¼ ounce can whole kernel corn, drained
1 10¾ ounce can cream of shrimp soup
1 15¾ ounce can cream corn
  salt and pepper to taste
  small amount of whipping cream for thinning or 1 cup half and half cream
1 cup green onions, chopped

Sauté onions in margarine until browned. Add bell pepper and sauté briefly until wilted. Add crabmeat, soups and corns. Add salt and pepper to taste. Add cream and bring to a slow simmer till ready to serve. Add green onions. Do not boil. Serves 4-6 bowls.

Notes

My Shrimp Creole

2 medium onions, finely chopped
½ cup prepared roux, dark brown
1 medium green pepper, finely chopped
¼ cup garlic, finely chopped
2 14 ounce cans stewed tomatoes or 1 can stewed tomatoes plus 1 can Rotel tomatoes
2 pounds peeled and deveined shrimp
  salt and pepper to taste
1 cup onion tops, chopped

I learned to cook this from my mama who learned from her mama. It was a very favorite meal for us on Fridays when we used to have to abstain from meat. To me that wasn't a penance at all.

Cook onions in hot roux until tender. Add bell pepper and garlic. Sauté briefly. Add tomatoes and cook on medium heat for 30 minutes. (If it cooks down too much and the sauce is too thick, add ½ cup water). Add shrimp and salt and pepper. Add onion tops. Cook for about 20 minutes or until shrimp are done (do not overcook shrimp). You may wish to also season with Louisiana Red Hot sauce; I do. Serve over rice. Serves 4-6.

NOTES

Chicken Stew

This was one of the favorite dishes I'd cook for the harvest crew. My brother-in-law Edmond especially loved this. I'd fix a huge pot of stew with rice and send them out to the field feeling pretty miserable because of overeating.

1   4-5 pound hen or 1 large fryer, cut into serving pieces
    salt and pepper to taste
½   cup flour
½   cup oil
1-2 quarts water
1   cup onion, chopped
½   cup bell pepper, chopped

Season chicken. Set aside. Brown flour in oil until chocolate colored. Add 1 quart water and bring to a rapid boil. Drop chicken pieces into pot; add onions and bell pepper. Cover and allow to slow boil till chicken is real tender. Stir occasionally and make sure the gravy doesn't get too thick. If it does get too thick, add small amounts of water until gravy gets the right consistency to serve over rice. Serves 6.

Smothered Calf Liver

I really like beef liver cooked like this. Mama fixed this for Daddy real often and that's when I cultivated a taste for it. At my husband's family they always had fried liver without the flour and served it over grits. We at my house, on the contrary, ate our smothered liver over rice. I cook this for Barbara, also.

1   pound calf liver
    salt and pepper to taste
1   cup flour
    oil to line bottom of pot
2   large onions, sliced
½   cup water

Coat seasoned liver with flour. Brown in hot oil in pot. Add sliced onions on top and water. Cover and allow to simmer for about 20 minutes. Serves 4.

Mama's Chicken Fricassee

1 4-5 pound hen, cut into serving
   pieces
   salt and pepper to taste
   oil to cover bottom of pot
4 cups water
2 large onions, chopped
1 large bell pepper, chopped
1 cup green onion tops, chopped

*Being we had our own
chicken, this was a
frequent meal on our
table. The gravy is out
of this world. And the
chicken melts in your
mouth. Mama was a
pro at this and I'm
still trying to cook it
as good as hers.*

Season chicken. Line heavy roaster with oil.
Heat. In hot oil, brown pieces of hen till well
browned on all sides. Keep turning to avoid
burning but allow to stick a little to bottom of
pot. Add water, onions and bell pepper and
cover. Allow to cook on medium heat for about
1½ hours, depending on how large the hen is.
Keep stirring occasionally and check to see if
extra water is needed. Just before done, add
onion tops and have enough water to make a
gravy. Cover and cook on low for 5-10 minutes.
Serve over rice. Serves 6.

NOTES

Chicken Jambalaya

This is another of my mama's real good dishes. We ate this quite often at home since we had access to all the ingredients right there in our yard. I still enjoy cooking this even though I don't have the pleasure of wringing the chicken's neck and plucking the feathers. That was the good old days!

1   **large hen or fryer, cut up into serving pieces**
     salt and pepper to taste
½   **cup oil**
3   **medium onions, chopped (1 cup)**
1   **cup bell pepper, chopped**
1   **cup celery, chopped**
½   **cup canned tomatoes (optional)**
3   **quarts water**
3   **cups cooked rice, cooled**
1   **cup green onions, chopped**

Season hen or fryer with salt and pepper. Brown in oil in a heavy pot. Remove browned pieces and most of oil. Add onions, bell pepper, celery, tomatoes and water. Bring to a boil, scraping all the crust off the bottom of the pot. Add the hen or fryer pieces and lower heat. Cover and cook until chicken is done and water has cooked down to make a real good gravy. You may need to cook uncovered for about 10 minutes before adding the rice. Then add cooked rice and chopped green onions, stirring well to make sure all is well mixed. Cover and simmer on low heat for about 10 minutes. Serves 6.

Chicken Fried Steak

2-3 **pounds round steak, tenderized**
salt and pepper to taste
3 **eggs, beaten**
3 **cups flour**
oil for frying, about ¼ inch bottom
of pot

Season round steaks, cut about 2-3 inches in length. Beat eggs in deep bowl or oblong dish. Run steaks through eggs, coating well, then dredge in flour, coating well. Lay in hot oil and fry on both sides till medium brown, turning as needed. You may need to lower fire to finish cooking the meat. Remove from pot and serve warm.

Rice dressing is always good with this. Or you may drain the oil out of pot which meat has browned, add a tablespoon of flour, salt and pepper, and some water or milk to form a gravy. Then serve over rice.

This is a great family dish! We all enjoy this every chance we get. What I like to eat with this is the rice dressing, of course, and, believe it or not, some whole fig preserves.

Blaise's Salad

1 **cup green onions, finely chopped**
1 **cup celery, finely chopped**
1 **cup bell pepper, finely chopped**
1 **15½ ounce can shoe peg corn,**
drained
1 **15 ounce can very small peas (petit**
pois)
½ **cup vinegar**
¼ **cup oil**
red hot sauce

My most precious friend, Blaise Domino, gave me this recipe. He loves to cook and does pretty good. This can be used as a vegetable or a salad with the meal.

Throw everything together and serve. Better if prepared the day before and refrigerated.

Boiled-Fried New Potatoes

6 **small or medium new potatoes**
   water to boil potatoes
1 **stick margarine**
   salt and pepper to taste

Harry's grandmother had this at every meal. She passed it down to our family. I fix these real often when the potatoes are just getting large enough to dig. I also use old potatoes but it doesn't seem to be as good.

Boil potatoes in their skins till done. Allow to cool. Peel and slice into about ¼ inch thick rounds. Heat heavy skillet and melt margarine. When hot, drop sliced potatoes in margarine and fry on each side till brown. Remove from skillet and season with salt and pepper. Serve hot. Serves 4.

Cajun-German Mustard Greens

2 **slices bacon, cut up**
1 **medium potato, diced**
1 **bundle fresh mustard greens, cut up**
   salt and pepper to taste
4 **ounces water**

My mother-in-law taught me how to cook good mustard greens. I think it's a combination of Cajun and German cuisine. Regardless, it is real good. We always cut the big stems off the leaves. Collard greens could also be used. I love to cook this but it takes a lot of mustard greens to make a little since they cook down so much.

In a 4 quart saucepan, brown bacon. Add diced potato and mustard greens which have been washed and cut up. Add water and cover. Cook on medium heat until mustard greens are well done. Season with salt and pepper. Take a pastry blender or potato masher and mash mustard greens well. Serve hot. Serves 4.

Baked Stuffed Potatoes

4 **baking potatoes**
   salt and pepper to taste
¼ **cup butter**
¼ **teaspoon onion salt**
1 **teaspoon garlic powder**
¼ **cup onion tops, chopped, for**
   topping

Wrap potatoes in foil. Bake at 400 degrees for 1 hour or until soft. Remove from oven. Unwrap. Cut each potato in halves. Scoop out the potatoes. Mash well. Season. Add butter, onion salt and garlic powder and mix well. Stuff the potato shells. Set aside until needed then bake at 350 degrees for 10 minutes. Top with finely chopped onion tops. Serve. Serves 8.

I learned how to prepare this when I needed baked potatoes to be hot upon serving the main dish. This is so simple that I sometimes fix this the day before, wrap them in foil and bake about 15 minutes before every other dish is ready. It's great because all you need to do is open up the foil and dig in!

String Bean Casserole

2 **14½ ounce cans string beans**
¾ **cup milk**
1 **15¾ ounce can cream of mushroom**
   soup
1 **1 ounce can fried onion rings**
   salt and pepper to taste

Spray a casserole with nonstick coating. Mix all ingredients together until well blended, using ¾ of onion rings. Pour into casserole and sprinkle the rest of onion rings on top. Cover and bake at 350 degrees for about 20 minutes or until warm. About 5 minutes before serving, uncover and allow onions to lightly brown. Serves 6.

This is not a Cajun casserole even though I'm sure many of us are using this recipe. It is very easy and quick to prepare and can be served with anything.

Tartar Sauce

We seldom use any cocktail or tartar sauce at home. So that's why I don't keep some made all of the time. But when I need some, I just whip up one of both of these two. Fresh horseradish is always best. And thanks to Charlie McKenzie, I keep some in my refrigerator all year.

1 cup mayonnaise
2 tablespoons sweet pickle relish
1 small onion, grated
1 tablespoon horseradish
 salt and pepper to taste

Mix all the above ingredients together thoroughly. Let stand at least 30 minutes before serving. Chill.

Seafood Cocktail Sauce

⅔ cup catsup
2 tablespoons horseradish
 juice of ½ fresh lemon
 Louisiana Red Hot Pepper sauce to taste
 salt and pepper to taste
¼ cup mayonnaise

Mix all the above thoroughly together. Serve cold with boiled or fried seafood.

Cooking Terms

Bake —To cook by dry heat, usually in an oven.

Baste — To moisten foods during cooking with pan drippings or a special sauce to add flavor and to prevent drying.

Beat — To make a mixture smooth by adding air with a brisk whipping or stirring motion, using a spoon or an electric mixer.

Blanch —To precook in boiling water or steam to prepare foods for canning or freezing, or to loosen their skins.

Blend — To process food in an electric blender. Or, to thoroughly combine two or more ingredients by hand with a stirring motion to make a smooth and uniform mixture.

Boil —To cook in liquid at boiling temperature where bubbles rise to the surface and break. For a full, rolling boil, bubbles form rapidly throughout the mixture.

Braise — To cook slowly with a small amount of liquid in a tightly covered pan on top of the range or in the oven.

Bread — To coat with bread crumbs before cooking.

Broil — To cook by direct heat, usually in a broiler or over coals.

Butterfly — To split foods such as shrimp and steak through the middle without completely separating sections and then spreading the sections to resemble a butterfly.

Caramelize — To melt sugar slowly over low heat until it becomes brown in color.

Chop — To cut into pieces about the size of peas with a knife, chopper, blender or food processor.

Coat — To evenly cover food with crumbs, flour or a batter.

Cream — To beat a mixture with a spoon or electric mixer till it becomes soft and smooth. When applied to combining shortening and sugar, the mixture is beaten till light and fluffy, depending on the proportion of sugar to shortening.

Crisp-tender —To cook food to the stage where it is tender but still crisp.

Cube — To cut into pieces that are the same size on each side — at least half an inch.

Cut in — To mix shortening with dry ingredients using a pastry blender or two knives.

Dab — A small amount; more than a dash.

Dash — ⅛ teaspoon of dry ingredients or liquids.

Dice — To cut food into small cubes of uniform size and shape — between ⅛ and ¼ inch.

Dredge — To coat with flour or sugar.

Dust —To sprinkle foods lightly with sugar, flour, etc.

Fillet — To cut lean meat or fish into pieces without bones.

Finely shred — To rub food across a fine shredding surface to form very narrow strips.

Fold — To add ingredients gently to a mixture. Using a spatula, cut down through the mixture; cut across the bottom of the bowl, and then up and over, close to the surface. Turn the bowl frequently for even distribution.

Fry — To cook in hot fat. To panfry, cook food in a small amount of fat. To deep-fat fry, cook the food immersed in a large amount of fat.

Grate — To rub food across a grating surface that separates the food into very fine particles.

Grill — To cook food over hot coals.

Grind — To use a food grinder to cut a food into very fine pieces.

Julienne — To cut vegetables, fruits or meats into matchlike strips.

Knead — To work dough with the heel of your hand in a pressing and folding motion.

Marinate — To allow a food to stand in a liquid to add flavor.

Mince — To chop food into very small, irregularly shaped pieces.

Mix — To stir together evenly.

Panbroil — To cook uncovered, removing fat as it accumulates.

Panfry — To cook food in a small amount of hot fat.

Peel — To remove the outer layer or skin from a fruit or vegetable.

Poach — To cook food in hot liquid, being careful that the food holds its shape while cooking.

Sauté — To brown or cook food in a small amount of hot fat.

Scald — To bring food to a temperature just below boiling so that tiny bubbles form at the edges of the pan.

Sear — To brown the surface of meat by quick application of intense heat, usually in a hot pot, pan or hot oven.

Shred — To rub food on a shredder to form long, narrow pieces.

Sift — To put one one or more dry ingredients through a sieve or sifter to incorporate air and break up lumps.

Simmer — To cook food in liquid over low heat at a temperature of 185-210 degrees F. (85-99 degrees C.) where bubbles form at a slow rate and burst before reaching the surface.

Sliver — To cut or shred into lengths.

Steam — To cook food in steam. A small amount of boiling water is used and more water is added during steaming if necessary.

Stew — To simmer cooked food slowly in a small amount of liquid.

Stir — To mix ingredients with a spoon in a circular or figure-eight motion till well combined.

Stir-fry — To cook food quickly in a small amount of hot fat, stirring constantly.

Toss — To mix ingredients lightly by lifting and dropping them with a spoon or a spoon and fork.

Whip — To beat food lightly and rapidly, incorporating air into the mixture to make it light and to increase volume.

Glossary

ANDOUILLE: A popular reddish Cajun pork sausage made from pork stomach and other ingredients.

APPETIZER: A snack.

BISQUE: A popular Cajun soup often made with crawfish, in which the crawfish heads are stuffed with meat of the tails and placed in the soup bowl.

BOUCHERIE: A great Cajun tradition whereby groups of families got together once a week to butcher one or more calves or pigs, thereafter dividing the various cuts and making various Cajun dishes such as boudin, hogshead cheese and cracklins from portions of the pigs.

BOUDIN: A popular Cajun pork sausage, usually light in color, made with rice and various parts of pork.

BRUNCH: Some meal that Cajuns do not have.

CAJUN MUSIC: Strictly Cajun French with one-step, two-step and jitterbug dancing. Bands consists of an accordian player, a guitar player, a violin player and a drummer. Sometimes a steel guitar player or vocalist who also plays an instrument, is added. (Cajun bands are mostly made up of family members.)

CORNICHON: Cucumber strips soaked in vinegar with hot peppers.

COURTBOUILLION: A light Cajun fish soup including tomatoes and served with rice.

CRACKLINS: A dish made by frying small cut portions of pork skin and pork fat; also called "gratons."

CRAWFISH: A plentiful Louisiana crustacean used in many classic Cajun dishes, which looks like a small lobster.

ETOUFFEE: A method of Cajun food preparation meaning smothered and cooked without a roux.

EXACT MEASUREMENTS: Just enough — not too much!

FILÉ: A ground sassafras leaf. Used to season and thicken gumbo. (Always add to gumbo just before it is served, preferably in a plate or bowl of gumbo.)

FRICASSEE: A Cajun stew made with a roux and chicken, duck, venison, beef or other meats and served over rice.

GREEN ONIONS: A very commonly used seasoning in Cajun dishes; also sometimes referred to as green onion tops by the Cajuns.

GUMBO: A soup or stew usually made with a roux and including meats commonly available in Cajun country, such as fowl, game, Cajun sausage, tasso, or seafoods.

JAMBALAYA: A Cajun dish in which pork, game and various other ingredients are cooked together with rice.

LAGNIAPPE: A French word meaning something extra or in addition to or including other things.

OKRA: A green pod vegetable of African origin used in gumbos and as a side dish.

PIROGUE: A small, narrow wooden boat resembling a canoe in structure, used in the bayou.

ROUX: A classic Cajun concoction made by blending flour and oil and cooking the two together; used in Cajun gumbos, stews fricassees, courtbouillons, sauce piquantes and other dishes.

SALT MEAT: A salty pork meat often used to season Cajun soups and other dishes.

SAUCE: A gravy.

SAUCE PIQUANT: A hot, spicy Cajun stew made with a roux, tomato sauce and various meats such as hen, geese, duck, rabbits, squirrel or turtle and other meats historically available in Cajun country.

SAUSAGE CASING: A natural casing used in the preparation of boudin, andouille and pork sausages made from the intestines of pork and beef and readily available at most meat markets.

TASSO: A dried, smoked pork used in gumbos and other dishes.

ZYDECO MUSIC: A blend of Cajun, jazz, rock, soul and country music creating a whole new style of dancing to a different beat.

This for That

INSTEAD OF THIS:	USE THIS:
1 clove fresh garlic	⅛ teaspoon garlic powder
1 tablespoon fresh herbs	1 teaspoon ground or crushed herbs
1 teaspoon lemon juice	½ teaspoon vinegar
1 teaspoon onion powder	2 teaspoons baking powder
BREAD CRUMBS	
1 cup bread crumbs	¾ cup cracker crumbs
BUTTER	
1 cup butter	1 cup margarine
	⅞ cup clarified bacon fat or drippings (for sautéing)
	⅞ cup lard or solid shortening
CHOCOLATE	
1 square	¼ cup cocoa
1 ounce square, unsweetened	3 tablespoons cocoa plus 1 tablespoon shortening
CREAM	
1 cup coffee cream	3 tablespoons butter plus ⅞ cup milk
1 cup heavy cream	⅓ cup butter plus ¾ cup milk
1 cup half and half	1½ tablespoon butter plus ⅞ cup milk
1 cup sour	1 tablespoon lemon juice plus plus evaporated milk to equal one cup
1 cup whipping	⅓ cup butter plus ¾ cup milk
FLOUR	
1 cup all purpose	1 cup plus 2 tablespoons cake flour
1 cup cake flour	⅞ cup all purpose flour
1 cup self-rising	1 cup all purpose plus 1 teaspoon baking powder and ½ teaspoon salt
1 tablespoon for thickening	½ tablespoon corn starch, potato starch or rice starch or 1 tablespoon tapioca
1 tablespoon corn starch	2 tablespoons flour (for thickening)
HONEY	
1 cup	1-1¼ cups sugar plus ¼ cup liquid
MILK	
1 cup fresh, whole	1 cup laso fat plus 2 tablespoons butter
1 cup whole	½ cup evaporated milk plus ½ cup water
1 cup skim	4 tablespoons nonfat dry milk plus 1 cup water
MUSHROOMS	
1 pound fresh	6 ounces canned mushrooms
SUGAR	
1 tablespoon maple	1 teaspoon white granulated sugar
1 cup maple	1 cup brown sugar
TOMATOES	
1 cup, packed	½ cup tomato sauce plus ½ cup water
1 cup, juice	½ cup tomato sauce plus ½ cup water
2 cups, sauce	¾ cup tomato paste plus 1 cup water
YEAST	
1 cake compressed	1 package or 2 teaspoons active dry yeast

Index

Classic CAJUN
P. O. Box 99
Dry Prong, LA 71423

Please send _____ copies of **Classic Cajun** @ $14.95 each _____
Postage and handling @ $ 2.00 each _____
Louisiana residents add sales tax @ $ 1.05 each _____
TOTAL _____

Name _____
Address _____

City _____ State _____ Zip _____

Make checks payable to **Classic Cajun**
Or Call 800/257-LUCY (5829)

- -

Classic CAJUN
P. O. Box 99
Dry Prong, LA 71423

Please send _____ copies of **Classic Cajun** @ $14.95 each _____
Postage and handling @ $ 2.00 each _____
Louisiana residents add sales tax @ $ 1.05 each _____
TOTAL _____

Name _____
Address _____

City _____ State _____ Zip _____

Make checks payable to **Classic Cajun**
Or Call 800/257-LUCY (5829)

- -

Classic CAJUN
P. O. Box 99
Dry Prong, LA 71423

Please send _____ copies of **Classic Cajun** @ $14.95 each _____
Postage and handling @ $ 2.00 each _____
Louisiana residents add sales tax @ $ 1.05 each _____
TOTAL _____

Name _____
Address _____

City _____ State _____ Zip _____

Make checks payable to **Classic Cajun**